# MEDITATIONAL THERAPY

Edited By
## Swami Ajaya

# MEDITATIONAL THERAPY

Edited By
## Swami Ajaya

Published by

Himalayan International Institute
of Yoga Science & Philosophy of USA

ISBN: 0-89389-032-4

Copyright 1977

HIMALAYAN INTERNATIONAL INSTITUTE
OF YOGA SCIENCE & PHILOSOPHY OF USA
1505 Greenwood Road, Glenview, IL 60025

# Contents

# Introduction

This is the third in a series of books which compare and integrate yoga and modern psychology. The first, *Psychology East and West*, dealt with yoga and modern techniques of psychotherapy. In the second, *Foundations of Eastern and Western Psychology*, the theoretical assumptions of yoga psychology and modern psychology were contrasted. This book, *Meditational Therapy*, shows how the applied science of yoga can be used in conjunction with modern methods to successfully treat the stress-related dysfunctions which are prevalent in our society.

The five chapters which comprise this book focus on the use of yoga and meditation in the treatment of stress, drug dependency, tension headaches, anxiety and a variety of psychosomatic dysfunctions. The clinical research described suggests that yoga and meditation in conjunction with other techniques which deal with the whole person can be remarkably successful in leading to the alleviation of psycho-physical disorders. In contrast to most other treatment methods which encourage dependency on external sources of regulation, this approach helps the individual to accept responsibility for himself and to alter the conditions that lead him to suffer.

The first chapter reviews research on stress and points out that meditation can change the way an individual reacts to stressful situations. The author further notes that meditation combined in a more holistic way with other yogic practices may prevent or minimize the occurrence of stress. Although meditation is traditionally a part of a more comprehensive approach, the research which has been conducted in the United States until now has almost exclusively considered it to be an isolated practice. Dr. Smith concludes that "the time is ripe for research to look at the effects of meditation with other procedures."

This review serves to introduce the next four chapters in this book. Each of the remaining chapters is a report of recent clinical experiments carried out by professionals associated with the Himalayan Institute. Each therapeutic program was carried out independently in different locals. However, they share the understanding that the most effective means of treating disorders and encouraging growth is a holistic approach which teaches the individual to assume responsibility for all aspects of his/her functioning. These studies clearly demonstrate the benefits of yoga and meditation when used in conjunction with other therapeutic methods in treating a variety of disorders.

Chapter two reports on the combined practice of hatha yoga postures, breathing, relaxation exercises and meditation. Significant positive changes in the way one experiences his/her body, and in one's level of anxiety are reported. The second phase of this research indicates that these practices are particularly effective in drug rehabilitation. Those who received the hatha yoga and meditation training experienced an increased sense of well-being which could be experienced without drugs and which seemed to make chemical dependency unnecessary. This study was carried out on a small group of subjects and a more expanded study is needed. But the results are significant and suggestive. Yoga and meditation may be one of the most effective means for curtailing chemical dependency.

The next chapter compares the effects of biofeedback and meditation in regulating one's level of arousal. While biofeedback is successful in increasing one's level of physiological functioning such as heart rate, its effect is not so clear in the other direction. But in treating anxiety and its related symptoms, a lowering of physiological functioning is sought. The author explores meditation as another means of self-regulation, and compares these two approaches in a series of experiments. While meditation is found to be more effective, the author points up the need for further study in a more clinical setting, using patients who are actually experiencing symptoms associated with anxiety. Chapter four provides us with such a study.

Chapter four focuses on the treatment of tension headaches and chronic anxiety. Dr. Nuernberger describes a training program which integrates meditation, yogic breathing and relaxation techniques, biofeedback and yoga-based counseling to teach self-awareness and self-regulation. Many of Dr. Nuernberger's patients had experienced disabling symptoms for several years, with little relief from other treatments they had received. With this approach many patients were able to achieve relief from their symptoms within less than six weeks.

The final chapter describes an even more comprehensive therapy program used at the Himalayan Institute to deal with a wide variety of psychosomatic disorders. Dr. Ballentine begins with the premise that the mind can control the body in all aspects. He then shows how this principle is applied in the innovative therapy program which he directs. He points out that while most Western medicines seek to *treat* the patient, yoga and other meditation-related therapies focus on *training*. The individual is taught to become more sensitive to his inner processes and to alter them through conscious control.

These studies point toward a new way in which we can regard ourselves and toward a new approach in the treatment of psychological and physical dysfunction. We are learning that we can become aware of the subtle functioning of our bodies, emotions and mental states and that we can learn to alter them directly, to become more relaxed, more effective and symptom-freed. Through self-regulation of our internal states we can achieve an enhanced sense of well-being that has not otherwise been possible.

Swami Ajaya
May 5, 1977

# Yoga and Stress

JONATHAN C. SMITH, Ph.D.

The ancient Indian scripture, the *Bhagavad Gita*, teaches that activity is inherent to life, and that all activity has consequences. Today we know that one pervasive physiological consequence of activity is stress. There is no life without stress. Yet stress affects how fully, healthily and effectively we live.

A first step in understanding yoga and its potential lies in examining its relationship to activity and stress. The *Gita* teaches that full authentic action is done in the spirit of yoga. In this paper I propose a related idea: yoga can both reduce the magnitude of stress and ameliorate its lingering, and at times destructive, consequences.

First, before considering yoga, we must devote some time to the nature and consequences of stress. For the sake of simplicity we shall consider only one aspect of stress—the nonspecific physiological accompaniment and consequence of life's changes and demands. Specifically, stress is: 1) the release of energy into an internal physiological system in preparation for activity, 2) the wear and tear that results from activity, and 3) the adaptive attempts at recooperation and defense that occur in response to bodily wear and tear.

Before one engages in any form of activity, he must be aroused and awakened; he must be "activated." Although activation is specific, affecting primarily the organ system to be used, it is also nonspecific, affecting virtually every organ system. An individual preparing for a fight may not only tighten or activate his fist, but his entire body—his heart, lungs, brain, etc.

The nonspecific quality of activation can be graphically illustrated in one, somewhat idealized, type of energization—Cannon's "fight or flight" defense alarm reaction. Cannon (1932) proposes that through natural selection we have developed an automatic, generalized response to threat, one that prepares the entire body for strong defensive exertion. Specifically, in response to a perceived threat, one experiences the following changes:

1. **Increased muscle tension.** Obviously when one prepares to fight or flee he will probably experience an increase in tension in the muscles that will be doing the fighting or fleeing. However, in addition to this specific form of muscle tension, some tension will likely appear in virtually every muscle group of the body. If you try making a tight fist, in a few

seconds you will note increased activation in other related muscles, those of the face, legs, arms, chest, and so on. Generalized muscle activation accompanies thought as well as physical activity. If you think of fighting, your fists will show some increments in activation.

2. **Increased palmar perspiration.** Perspiration is, of course, the body's way of coping with excess heat. In addition perspiration in certain parts of the body such as the palms is an adaptive component of the defense alarm reaction. A slightly moist palm increases the firmness of one's grip, making it less likely that one will drop a club, rock, or getaway rope. Perspiration also makes the skin more sensitive and less easily cut.

3. **Increased heart rate.** As the heart beats more quickly it makes available additional blood supplies of sugar and oxygen for defensive activity.

4. **Dilation of arteries to large muscle groups.** With dilated arteries, blood can flow more easily to areas in greatest need.

5. **Increased adrenalin secretion.** Adrenalin is one of several hormones that has a general activating effect; its secretion therefore reinforces all the components of activation.

6. **Increased breath rate.** As the organism's demand for sugar increases, breathing must increase to supply the oxygen needed for metabolism, and to remove the by-products of metabolism.

7. **Increased brain wave activity.** For many people relatively slow alpha brain wave activity is blocked. The proportion of faster beta wave activity, activity associated with active concentration, increases.

We have spent considerable space describing non-specific activation, particularly Cannon's defense alarm reaction. We have done this for two reasons. First, the changes listed are precisely those which occur in the first phases of meditation, only in the reverse direction. And second, excessive activation can be harmful to health, and can reduce one's ability to work on complex tasks demanding flexibility and originality. In today's pressured society activation may be triggered more often than is desirable. Charvat, Dell and Folkow (1964) speculate that in civilized society symbolic dangers repeatedly activate the defense alarm reaction. Although this reaction is ideal for supporting violent physical exertion, physical exertion is rarely an appropriate consequence to symbolic threat. Thus, exertion does not occur, the somatomotor component (fighting or fleeing) of the defense alarm reaction is suppressed, and the visceral and endocrine components linger. These may ultimately contribute to such problems as heart disease and hypertension.

Not only does activity demand energizing activation, but it produces bodily wear and tear and triggers physiological attempts at recooperation and defense. Hans Selye has devoted much of his life to studying the mechanisms behind wear and tear and repair. His conclusions can be stated simply (Selye, 1977): 1) all change, both good and bad, triggers a "stress mechanism" involving primarily the hypothalamus, pituitary gland, and the adrenal cortex, 2) this stress mechanism, like activation, affects the entire body, and 3) the stress mechanism when activated over a period of time, progresses through a series of changes leading to exhaustion.

Activation of the stress mechanism is costly. When using one's physiological resources to meet one stressor, fewer resources are available for coping with other stressors and one may, for example, be more susceptible to disease. Also, every stressful experience depletes to a small extent one's adaptive resources. As Selye puts it:

> Experiments on animals have clearly shown that each exposure leaves an indelible scar, in that it uses up reserves of adaptability which cannot be replaced. It is true that immediately after one harassing experience, rest can restore us almost to the original level of fitness by eliminating acute fatigue. But the emphasis is on almost. Since we constantly go through periods of stress and rest, just a little deficit of adaption energy every day adds up—it adds up to what we call aging.

What we have said to this point can be summarized briefly: life's changes and demands produce stress, and stress can be harmful. I want to end this discussion on stress by sharing one experiment that illustrates the costs of stress far more convincingly than could a lecture on physiology.

If change is stressful, and stress can increase the

incidence of disease, then individuals who experience a great deal of change should also display a high susceptibility to disease. To examine the possibility, Holmes & Rahe (1967) first designed a questionnaire to measure experienced life change. The result, the Social Readjustment Rating Questionnaire, (the SRRQ), lists 42 items depicting various life changes involving modifications in sleeping, eating, social, recreational, personal, and interpersonal habits. Items range from "vacation" and "change in recreation" to "pregnancy" and "divorce." Each item is weighted according to the amount, severity, and duration of adjustment each is perceived to require, so that "vacation," for example, receives a low weight and "pregnancy" receives a high weight. A person taking the questionnaire receives one score, the sum of the weights of the life changes he has experienced over a period of time.

In another phase of this research (Rahe, Mahan & Arthur, 1970) versions of the SRRQ were given to 2463 enlisted Navy men before their ships left for various six to eight month overseas cruises. At the end of each cruise the amount of illness experienced during the cruise was correlated with the amount of life change experienced before the cruise. The results were startling. During the first month of the cruise period, those who experienced the most life change prior to the cruise (the top 30%) experienced 90% more first illnesses than those who experienced less life change (the bottom 30%). Furthermore, those who experienced more life change also experienced more severe illnesses.

## Yoga and the Consequences of Stress

Meditation is an aspect of yoga that involves calmly limiting attention to a restricted stimulus. The relationship between meditation and stress is simple: physiologically they appear to be mirror opposites. In meditation one experiences a decrease in metabolic activity, brain wave activity, and a constellation of other changes in the opposite direction of nonspecific activation, or Cannon's fight or flight reaction (Wallace & Benson, 1972). In addition the changes characteristic of meditation are in the opposite direction of those characteristic of the wear, tear, and repair of stress (Selye, 1977).

As an antistress technique, meditation may have considerable use for reducing the lingering consequences of stress. Selye proposes that if one is repeatedly presented with the same kind of problem again and again, his bodily stress reactions may become stereotyped so that they "fall into a groove, for instance, by always responding with the same exaggerated hormonal response, whether it is appropriate to the situation or not." Meditation, Selye suggests, provides a "complete rest, which gives the body time to ' forget ' stereotyped somatic reactions to stress." In addition, one may also become habitually attached to experiencing the stress reaction, or as Selye puts it, "intoxicated with his own stress hormones." Meditation may enable one to break out of this habit. Finally, one may experience a series of changes and demands with little intervening vacation time for stress to dissipate. Stress may well accumulate, and sensitize one to experience even more stress. Meditation may again be a way out of such a driven and destructive pattern of living.

Goleman (Goleman & Schwartz, 1976) provides some support for the potential of meditation as a stress-coping technique. He exposed subjects to a somewhat gruesome stressor, a film depicting workshop accidents in which, among other things, one worker has his finger cut off, and an innocent bystander is killed by a wooden plank driven through his midsection as a result of carelessness by a circle-saw operator. After viewing this film, two measures of activation were taken, phasic skin conductance activity and heart rate, and rate of habituation or recovery to the film was observed. Experienced meditators and nonmeditators participated in the experiment. Some meditated before the film, while some simply sat with eyes closed or eyes open.

One result is particularly relevant. Meditators, regardless of what they did prior to the film, recovered more quickly than the nonmeditators. In addition, subjects who practiced meditation immediately before the stressor (subjects included experienced meditators and nonmeditators taught on the spot) recovered more quickly than meditator and nonmeditator subjects who did not meditate. Although this study is limited by a number of technical and interpretive difficulties, it does lend support to our proposal that meditation can reduce the stressful consequences of an event.

## Yoga and the Antecedents of Stress

We have been considering only the consequences of stress and ways of limiting these consequences after stressful activation has been triggered. However, it is also important to examine the antecedents of stress, variables that can affect whether a stress reaction occurs, and the magnitude with which it does occur. Meditation may not only enable one to get over stress once it occurs, but it may serve as a sort of stress-innoculation, and prevent or minimize its occurence.

All of us experience life's changes. However, for some even minor irritation, such as a stalled car, or a cancelled television program, can be a minor catastrophy. Others seem to take major trials and tribulations in stride, suffering little from their impact. Cognitive and emotional factors, one's thoughts and feelings, appear to play a crucial role in mediating the stressful impact of change.

It is difficult to isolate one simple cognitive factor, one simple attitude or belief, that is most responsible for rendering change stressful. One can argue that appraisal of change as threatening or benign is of crucial importance (Lazarus, 1966). Another factor may be the degree to which one sees himself as helpless or lacking control (Seligman, 1975; Singer & Glass, 1972). However, I suspect that one's placement of values contributes much to what he experiences as stressful. A person who values achievement may feel threatened, helpless, and stressed when he does not receive an expected raise. A person who lives and strives for acquiring possessions may find material loss particularly stressful.

Those who take yoga seriously, and practice it rigorously, at times show profound changes in how they view and value themselves and the universe. Such changes in philosophy of life may well differ in content, reflecting the diversity of traditions underlying various schools of yoga. However, one finds in common such metaphors as "detachment," "transcendence," "surrender," "ego death," and letting go." Such metaphors point to a fundamental cognitive change, one in which life's changes are valued as having truly secondary or passing importance. I suspect that when a practitioner of yoga grows to experience change in such a spirit of detachment, he greatly reduces the stressful impact of change.

A person suffering from emotional difficulties, particularly anxiety, is more likely to be sensitized to irritations and frustrations; he is more likely to find life stressful (Cattell & Scheier, 1961). In fact, one major personality test of anxiety includes as one of its subtests a simple count of the number of situations one finds annoying (Cattell & Scheier, 1960).

For decades, scholarly arguments have appeared stating that meditation is, in and of itself, a "cure" for anxiety (Smith, 1975).

Unfortunately, research on TM and related experimental techniques does not support this conclusion. No fewer than four separate studies have compared meditation with various control procedures, for example, with sitting and reading, sitting and effortfully thinking thoughts, or just sitting (Marlatt & Marques, 1976; Otis: 1974; Smith, 1976). In every single study the meditation procedures were no more effective in reducing anxiety than some form of sitting. I conclude from such studies that TM and related techniques in and of themselves appear to have little general psychotherapeutic value.

However, I do propose that in a therapy setting, and in combination with traditional psychotherapy, biofeedback, or hatha yoga, meditation may have value for individuals suffering from acute anxiety and phobias. I base my thinking on a number of points. First, acutely anxious and phobic patients appear to respond well to fairly straightforward behavioral relaxation treatments which bear some resemblance to meditation (Coleman, 1976; Shapiro & Zifferblatt, 1976). Second, such behavioral treatments appear to be most effective when presented one-to-one in a personalized therapy setting. Third, relatively concrete disciplines, such as progressive relaxation, hatha yoga, and biofeedback may facilitate the acquisition of such skills as attending to a task, and noting and "letting go" of areas of skeletal muscle tension. Such skills are useful when learning and practicing the relatively subtle discipline of meditation.

The time is ripe for researchers to look at the effects of meditation in combination with other procedures. I know of only one study that has made such a comparison. However, this study is of such surpassing elegance that I think it merits detailed description. A group of researchers headed by N. S. Vahia (1973) at King Edward VI Memorial Hospital in Bombay, India wished to evaluate the effects of an experimental therapy, "psychophysiological therapy," a yoga treatment based on the concepts of Patanjali. Specifically, psychophysiological therapy incorporates five steps: 1) *asana*, or "the practice of certain selected postures for relaxation of the voluntary musculature," 2) *pranayama*, or "breathing practices for voluntary control of inspiration, expiration, and retention of breath," 3) *pratyahara*, or "restraint of the senses by voluntary withdrawal from the external environment," 4) *dharana* or "the selection of an object for concentration and development of increasing concentration on that object, with decreasing preoccupation with external stimuli," and 5) *dhyana* or the "development of integration with the selected object to the complete exclusion of all other thought processes and later, identification of that object with the integrating mechanism present within all of us leading to unison with it." In other words, psychophysiological therapy involves first learning hatha yoga postures, then breathing exercises and then meditation.

Ninety-five neurotic patients who displayed no improvement in response to previous therapy were randomly divided into carefully matched groups. One was given complete psychophysiological therapy, while the other was given a mock-yoga control treatment consisting of exercises resembling yoga exercises and no meditation. Both groups practiced one hour each weekday for 4-6 weeks, and were given support, reassurance, and placebo tablets.

In the tradition of rigorous psychotherapy outcome research, a variety of measures were given:    1) blind clinical assessment before, after, and every week of the project;    assessment focused on target symptom relief and work efficiency on the job as reported by the patients themselves, their relatives, friends, and colleagues;    2) daily notebooks written by all subjects on thoughts that came to mind while practicing;    3) the MMPI and Rorschach tests given before and after the project;    and 4) the Taylor Manifest Anxiety Scale given before, after, and every week of the project.

The results were striking.    On virtually every measure the yoga-meditation subjects improved more than the mock-yoga subjects.    Furthermore, the yoga-meditation subjects who displayed a greater ability to passively concentrate in meditation improved more than those who had difficulty meditating.    Meditation may well be effective and therapeutic when preceded by simpler "body" disciplines.

Vahia and his colleagues offer some speculation as to the therapeutic processes underlying psychophysiological therapy.    Interestingly they emphasize the importance of both emotional and cognitive factors in mediating stress.    Their words aptly summarize what I have to say in this paper:

> In a constantly changing environment, recurrent cycles of pleasure and pain are unavoidable.    The only way to maintain freedom from anxiety and its consequences under different kinds of life situations

is by unlearning being preoccupied with externally oriented pleasure and pain and relearning to channelize mental and physical faculties in an optimum fashion according to one's intrinsic capacities.

The basic concept of this therapy is to develop an ability not to respond to stress by the instinctual urge to "fight or flight" or any of its modifications, but to objectively assess the stress situation and act accordingly. The shift is from primary preoccupation with the environment to unattached objective assessment of the situation.

### References

Canon, J. The *Wisdom of the Body*. New York: Norton, 1932.

Cattell, R.B. & Scheier, I.H. *Handbook and Test Kit for the Objective-Analytic Anxiety Battery*. Champaign, Illinois: The Institute for Personality and Ability Testing, 1960.

Cattell, R.B. & Scheier, I.H. *The Meaning and Measurement of Neuroticism and Anxiety*. New York: The Ronald Press, 1961.

Charvat, J., Dell, P., Folkow, B. "Mental Factors and Cardiovascular Disorders," *Cardiologia*, 1964, 44, 124.

Goleman, D. "Meditation and Consciousness: An Asian Approach to Mental Health," *American Journal of Psychotherapy*, 1976, 30, 41-54.

Goleman, D. & Schwartz, G.E. "Meditation as an Intervention in Stress Reactivity," *Journal of Consulting and Clinical Psychology*, 1976, 44, 456-466.

Holmes, T. H. & Rahe, R. H. "The Socail Readjustment Rating Scale," *Journal of Psychosomatic Research*, 1967, 11, 213.

Lazarus, R.S. *Psychological Stress and the Coping Process*. New York: McGraw-Hill, 1966.

Marlatt, G.A. & Marques, J.K. *Meditation, Self-Control, and Alcohol Use*. Paper presented at the Eight Banff International Conference on Behavior Modification, Banff, Alberta, March, 1976.

Otis, L.S. "If Well-integrated but Anxious, Try TM," *Psychology Today*, April 1974, 45-46.

Rahe, R.H., Mahan, J.I., and Arthus, R.J. "Prediction of Near-Future Health Change from Subjects' Preceding Life Changes," *Journal of Psychosomatic Medicine*, 1970, 14, 401-406.

Seligman, M.E.P. *Helplessness.* San Francisco: W. H. Freeman & Co., 1975.

Selye, H. *The Stress of Life.* New York: McGraw-Hill, 1977.

Shapiro, D.H. & Zifferblatt, S.M. "Zen Meditation and Behavioral Self-Control," *American Psychologist*, 1976, 31, 5-9-532.

Singer, J. & Glass, D.C. "Behavioral Aftereffects of Unpredictable and Uncontrollable Aversive Events," *American Scientist*, 1972, 457-465.

Smith, J.C. "Meditation as Psychotherapy: A Review of the Literature," *Psychological Bulletin*, 1975, 82, 558-564.

Smith, J.C. "Psychotherapeutic Effects of Transcendental Meditation with Controls for Expectation of Relief and Daily Sitting," *Journal of Consulting and Clinical Psychology*, 1976, 44, 630-637.

Vahia, N.S., Donngaji, D.R., Jeste, D.V., Kapoor, S.N., Arhapurkar, I. and Ravindranath, S. "Further Experience with the Therapy Based Upon Concepts of Patanjali in the Treatment of Psychiatric Disorders," *Indian Journal of Psychiatry*, 1973, 15, 32-37.

Wallace, R.K. & Benson, H. "The Physiology of Meditation," *Scientific American*, 1972, 226, 84-90.

# Effects of Hatha Yoga and Meditation on Anxiety and Body Image

TIMOTHY J. THORPE, Ed.D.

The goals and methods of applied psychology are as diverse as the theories which attempt to explain the nature of man and the dynamics of his change. Within contemporary counseling and psychotherapy, numerous variations on the themes of behaviorism, psychoanalysis and humanism form the basis for most all theory and technique. Also, as part of the "human potential movement" within psychology, serious interest is emerging in yoga as a philosophy of man and system of psychophysical therapy. As a philosophy, yoga offers a transcendent vision of man wherein personal suffering and limitation can be transcended to a degree rarely considered realistic within theoretical psychology. As a method of psychophysical therapy, the techniques of hatha yoga and meditation are being increasingly investigated within education, medicine, and psychology. Technological advances in electronics are being applied to the measurement of psychophysical states and the educational and therapeutic benefits of these techniques are being confirmed by competent and responsible scientific inquiry. Claims that yoga is an occult or religious phenomena unworthy of scientific investigation are being voiced less frequently then in even the recent past.

Testimonials acclaiming the positive and powerful effects of hatha yoga and meditation abound, but from the perspective of the research psychologist, better designed studies need to be carried out to specify more explicitly what these effects might be. While the practitioner may believe that yoga practices are ultimately valuable only to the extent to which they are subjectively experienced, it can also be recognized that scientific verification of the effects could lead to their inclusion within the academic curriculums of teachers, physicians and psychologists. The integration of applied yoga practices with the objective, scientific methods of western science should not be understood as a desacralization of the ancient practices. Rather, the ability of yoga to adapt to a broad spectrum of cultural systems during the past 2,400 years speaks directly to its perennial utility.

Prior psychological research on yoga has focused on 1) the theoretical relationship between yoga and the different systems of Western psychology, 2) the physiology of meditation and the physiology of hatha yoga, 3) clinical observations of hatha yoga and meditation, and 4) the effects of hatha yoga and meditation as measured by psychological tests.

The theoretical comparisons between yoga psychology and Western psychology have been quite fruitful.

Abraham Maslow, renowned humanist and past president of the American Psychological Association went so far as to view yoga and related philosophies and methods as a new, fourth major trend within psychology.[1]   He called this trend "transpersonal psychology." Sidney Jourard saw yoga psychology as compatible with humanistic psychology in that they are both psychologies of health rather than sickness.[2]

Psychoanalyst Harchand Brar views the goals of yoga psychology and psychoanalysis to be highly similar.[3] They both seek to integrate the unconscious and conscious facets of personality and thereby increase the mental health of the individual. Psychoanalytic theory does not, however, recognize the existence of a superconscious or transcendent level of consciousness while yogic theory does.

The methods of behavioral psychology are also compatible with applied yoga because both seek to produce states of deep relaxation. Psychiatrist Joseph Wolpe teaches patients to relax deeply and then has them practice this relaxation in situations which usually disturb them.[4] Similarly, the methods of hatha yoga and meditation aim to bring the individual's level of relaxation under conscious control. Psychologists Deane Shapiro and Steven Zifferblatt, in a recent article in the *American Psychologist*, point out that meditation and newly developed behavioral self-control techniques are highly alike in that both demand high degrees of self-observation to produce desired changes.[5]   They also suggest that these techniques could be used simultaneously and thereby potentiate the effects of one upon the other.

Research on the physiology of meditation has identified the internal and external conditions of successful meditation as well as the highly specific and reliable effects upon physiological functioning. Harvard cardiologist Herbert Benson has shown that successful meditation may occur with 1) a quiet environment free of external distraction, 2) a comfortable, preferably seated position with the eyes closed, 3) the mental repetition of a sound or word in synchronization with the normal rhythm of the breath for at least 10 to 20 minutes`and 4) a passive "let it happen" attitude to thoughts which distract from the sound or word repetition.[6]  Predictable physiological changes during the meditation period include reduced oxygen consumption, respiratory rate, blood lactate (associated with anxiety), heart rate and blood pressure in those suffering from high blood pressure. Alpha waves increase in intensity and frequency. Physiologically the body is in a deeply relaxed or hypometabolic state while the mind remains alert. Benson calls this pattern of physiological activity the "relaxation response." He views it as an innate physiological state which counteracts the "flight or fight" response that is associated with states of anxiety, fear and anger.

An extensive study conducted at Benaras Hindu University showed that the regular practice of hatha yoga also increases physiological stress competence.[7]  Twelve young males undergoing a six-month, daily training program in hatha yoga showed a distinct enhancement of endocrinological and metabolic functioning which included increased 17-hydroxicorticosteriod excretion with reductions in blood levels of cholesterol and glucose and an increase in protein levels. The urinary excretion of testosterone also increased. This improved pattern of performance was further indicated through reductions in body weight and a significantly improved pattern of respiratory functions including lowered rate of respiration, increased rate of chest expansion and increased vital capacity and breath-holding time. EEG studies on these men showed increased alpha waves with fewer spikes, interpreted as a "less irritable nervous system."

Psychiatric researchers N. S. Vahia, S. L. Vinekar, and D. R. Doongaji reported using hatha yoga and meditation as therapy with psychiatric patients.[8] Of 30 patients suffering from anxiety, depression, and/or psychosomatic complaints, 26 showed a marked reduction in symptoms. Repeatedly it has been observed that individuals commencing the practice of meditation reduce or totally discontinue drug abuse. Herbert Benson and Keith Wallace reported significant reductions in the use of alcohol, amphetamines, marijuana, LSD, other hallucinogens, narcotics, and cigarettes for 1,862 students meditating for an average of 20 months.[9] Mohammed Shaffi, Richard Lavely, and Robert Jaffee, in the *American Journal of Psychiatry*, reported a positive relationship between the number of months meditating and the discontinuance of marijuana use.[10] These clinical observations suggest that hatha yoga and meditation could be of use as an adjunct in the treatment of common psychiatric syndromes. Numerous psychological tests have been used to assess the effects of hatha yoga and meditation. K. N. Udupa and R. H. Singh reported improved memory quotients, lowered rate of mental fatigability and decreased neuroticism in the 12 males undergoing the six month training in hatha yoga although the actual tests used were not reported. Philip Ferguson and John Gowan showed that self-reports of anxiety decrease significantly in relation to the number of months meditating as measured by the Spielberger Anxiety Inventory and IPAT Anxiety Scale Questionnaire.[11]    Using the Northridge Developmental Scale these same researchers demonstrated that depression and neuroticism also decreased significantly in relation to the number of months meditating. Using the Minneosta Multiphasic Personality Inventory (MMPI), David Orme-Johnson showed that the hypochondria, schizophrenia and anxiety scales significantly decreased in persons meditating for several months.[12]

Measurements on the Personal Orientation Inventory (POI) showed that self-actualization was affected in a positive manner through meditation.[13, 14] Inner directedness, time competence, existentiality, acceptance of aggression, self-regard, feeling reactivity, self-acceptance, capacity for intimate contact, self-actualizing value and spontaneity all increased after 10 weeks of meditation. Karen Blasdell demonstrated that meditators perform more quickly and accurately on a complex perceptual-motor test (Mirror Star-Tracing Test)[15] and John Graham showed that meditators have increased refinement in auditory discrimination.[16]  William Linden demonstrated that children taught to meditate were more "field independent" than a similar group of children who were not taught to meditate.[17]  That is, they learned to focus and refocus attention and disregard intrusions of distracting stimuli on the Children's Embedded Figures Test.

The overall review of the effects of hatha yoga and meditation suggests that the regular practice of one or both of these techniques produces fundamental physiological changes indicative of increased relaxation, stability, and self-control.  These physiological changes are reflected on a psychological level in reports of decreased anxiety and related symptoms, enhanced motor and perceptual acuity and improved progress toward self-actualization. How does this improved pattern of physiological functioning become manifest on the psychological level?

The most immediately experienced effects of hatha yoga and/or meditation are bodily ones.  The practitioner *experiences* changes in muscle tension, breath rate and circulatory activity.  There is an increased awareness of many different patterns of bodily sensation.  For example, as the attention focuses on the breath during meditation or rest intervals during hatha yoga, a very subtle pattern of sensation may be discovered consisting of a movement up from the diaphragm to the collar bones during inhalation with the opposite movement during exhalation.  This, and other patterns of sensation are increasingly discovered during the practice of hatha yoga and meditation. As the underlying physiological activity becomes more relaxed, stable and self-controlled, the sensation of self becomes more pleasant. The regular occurrence of such patterns of sensation through the yoga practices also enhances the fine control of movement and perception. Experienced satisfaction with the body, referred to as body image, becomes enhanced.

It is often the case that students new to hatha yoga and meditation experience themselves in a positive way for the first time in their lives as they increase awareness of these basic patterns of pleasurable sensation. As the body image becomes enhanced through the experience of more relaxed and stable physiological patterns, a more peaceful and secure self-concept is developed. Less anxiety, depression, psychosomatic disease, and drug dependence occurs along with increased self-actualization.

To further assess and evaluate the effects of hatha yoga and meditation on body image and anxiety, the present study was initiated and a questionnaire was constructed. The questionnaire consisted, first, of a large number of open ended questions allowing yoga students to indicate, in their own words, the effects of hatha yoga and meditation. The second part of the questionnaire consisted of a checklist of physical dysfunctions which included poor sleep, fatigue, headaches, body aches, spine curvature, poor vision, poor hearing, nervousness, stiff joints, overweight, underweight, indigestion, cigarette smoking, alcohol dependency and a

category to be filled in by the student entitled "other."
The students simply checked those dysfunctions which
existed prior to their practice of hatha yoga and meditation and those which improved or were eliminated through
their practice. Questionnaires were sent to several yoga
centers in the United States and Canada which offered
classes in hatha yoga and meditation.

In the seventy-five questionnaires which were
completed, the most striking results were reports of
decreased anxiety and improved physical health. All
respondents reported decreased anxiety. Phrases such as
"not so tense," "less uptight," "worry less," "more
calm," and "more relaxed" characterized all the returned questionnaires. "Nervousness" was included on
the physical dysfunction checklist and a clear result was
obtained. Every respondent reported they suffered from
nervousness prior to the practice of hatha yoga and meditation and every respondent reported they suffered from it
less as a result of their practice.

Clear results were also obtained on the other
symptoms listed on the physical dysfunction checklist.
The more months or years the respondents reported practicing hatha yoga and meditation the more likely they
reported a reduction or elimination of the effects of poor
sleep, fatigue, headaches, body aches, spine curvature,
poor vision, poor hearing, stiff joints, overweight, underweight, indigestion, smoking cigarettes and drinking alcohol. Some respondents also reported relief from a variety
of other complaints. They were sexual frustration (1),

laziness (1), menstrual cramps (2), diabetes (1), colds (1), migraine (1), drug dependence (5), asthma (1), allergies (3), constipation (1), hypoglycemia (1), kidney malfunction (1) and aging (1).

Along with reports of decreased anxiety and improved physical health there were reports of increased energy of vitality and enhanced spirituality or transcendence. Respondents reported that as they became more relaxed and healthy they spontaneously had more energy and interest in themselves and for others. Statements reporting a growing awareness of states of being or consciousness other than the ordinary were frequently voiced by those who had been practicing hatha yoga and meditation for more than a year.

To further clarify the effects of hatha yoga and meditation on anxiety and body image, a second, more experimental part of the study was designed and carried out. Although the first part of the study did indicate that hatha yoga and meditation decreased anxiety and physical dysfunction, there were inadequacies in the study demanding the subsequent use of a precisely described technique and the inclusion of a control group practicing similar activities.

Eleven patients residing at an inpatient drug-rehabilitation community on the grounds of a state psychiatric hospital received a lecture and demonstration of hatha yoga and meditation. Eight of the patients agreed to take part in the study but three dropped out during the first week. The five remaining patients, ranging in age from

18-49, participated in an intensive program of hatha yoga and meditation held five times a week for four consecutive weeks with each session lasting 90 minutes.

The overall goal of the drug rehabilitation community was to assist the patients in developing more responsible means of living.  To this end a highly structured program was in effect 24 hours a day which included individual, family, group, occupational and milieu therapy, academic/vocational counseling and remedial classes, gym period, "time alone" and shared responsibility for housekeeping.  The highly demanding nature of this program resulted in a patient population seldom exceeding 15 and was partly responsible for the low number of experimental participants in the study.

The particular components of this 90 minute class were hatha yoga poses for 45 minutes, guided relaxation for 15 minutes, breathing exercises (*pranayama*) for 15 minutes and meditation for 15 minutes.

Prior to the first yoga class and after the twentieth and final class the participants took two psychological tests.  They were the Body-Cathexis Scale[18] and the IPAT Anxiety Scale Questionnaire.[19]  The Body-Cathexis Scale had the participants rate, on a seven point scale, how satisfied or dissatisfied they were with 40 of their body parts plus overall physical appearance.  A body part would be rated a +3 if the participant had strong positive feelings about it, a +2 for moderately positive feelings, a +1 for slightly positive feelings, a 0 for neutral feelings, a -1 for slightly negative feelings, a -2 for moderately negative feelings and a -3 for strong negative feelings. The 40 body parts which were rated in this manner included the hair, hands, nose, sex organs, waist, back, ears, chin, skin texture, buttocks, ankles, neck, body build, profile, thighs, shoulder width, arms, chest or breasts, eyes, hips, lips, legs, feet, knees, posture, face and weight.

The IPAT Anxiety Scale Questionnaire assesses anxiety by asking direct true or false questions concerning the presence of a wide variety of anxious feelings and behaviors. It is a highly accurate test that tends to rank people on this level of anxiety as do psychiatrists.

The five participants were also evaluated on their behavior each week as a part of normal procedures at the drug community. If the majority of staff and other patients thought that a given patient had strived to maintain a positive attitude toward self, others and community during the prior week, that patient received a *Pass* evaluation and was advanced in standing toward discharge from the hospital. If the majority of staff and other patients did not think that a given patient had kept a positive attitude, she/he was given a *Fail* evaluation and standing toward discharge was not advanced. Neither the staff nor the patients were aware that the evaluations were being used in this study.

The results of the psychological tests and behavioral evaluations of the five patients who learned hatha yoga and meditation were compared to another group of ten patients who entered the treatment programs at a later date and served as a control group. The 15 patients on the unit at that time were presented with the lecture and demonstration of hatha yoga and meditation and 10 agreed to participate in the study  During the control period of four weeks these participants had a 60 minute gym and 30 minute "alone time" period five times a week for four weeks.  During the gym period they received instruction in and were allowed to play volleyball, basketball, gymnastics, swimming, football or tennis according to their desires.  During the 30 minute "alone time" period they were allowed to disengage from communal activities.  It was felt that the combination of gym and free time would represent an activity that, from appearances, was similar to hatha yoga and meditation.

The results were very clear.  The hatha yoga and meditation group reduced their anxiety significantly more than the gym and "alone time" group during the four weeks of their activities.  Despite the small sample size, the likelihood that the differences between the groups occurred by chance was less than three per cent ($p < .03$). The hatha yoga and meditation group also had significantly greater body-cathexis than the control group, with a less than one per cent chance that the result was due to chance ($p < .01$).  These statistical results were determined using an analysis of covariance test.

There also was a large difference between the groups on the weekly behavioral evaluations.  All five hatha yoga and meditation participants passed each weekly evaluation during the four weeks, giving them a score of 100%.  By contrast, the gym and "alone time" group had a score of only 65% *Pass* evaluations.

The participants in the hatha yoga and meditation group were also given a ten question, structured interview following their last class. They were asked short, open ended questions such as "What is the main change you have noticed about yourself since starting yoga?" or "Do you notice any differences in the way you act toward other people?"

Without exception these participants considered their involvement with hatha yoga and meditation to be a positive experience. They felt that they learned new and important ways to experience themselves and others. The ability to relax was the most apparent of these new experiences. Statements such as "I've never been so relaxed in my life as when I'm in deep relaxation " and "It's more like total relaxation to me than I've ever known before " characterize the responses of all the participants.

Along with the ability to relax deeply, the participants reported an increased functioning and appreciation of their bodies, indicative of enhanced body image. They experienced their bodies in ways that increased their overall feelings of worth, confidence and optimism. Examples of increased physical functioning and body image include "I'll get up in the morning and go out and I'm jumping all day—I really feel good " and "I feel better physically and I don't seem to gain weight as fast as I used to and I'm not as creaky in my joints . . . I'm a lot more graceful."

Although the sample in this study were drug users, there was no attempt to estimate treatment effects on drug taking behavior. However, the experimental participants all made reference to the possibility that the hatha yoga and meditation produced experiences which could serve as healthy substitutes for drug use. Some statements include "Outwardly I get a big smile on my face. People say I look stoned but I don't feel stoned—I just feel good." "I don't think I'll ever go back to hard drugs if I keep this feeling." and "If I get back on the streets and get real depressed I hope that I can do yoga and get the feeling I want rather than resorting back to drugs."

Finally, it may be noted that the participants frequently expressed a difficulty finding words to describe the experiences associated with hatha yoga and meditation. An initial possibility is that this difficulty reflects the generally low educational level of young adult drug users. A second explanation is that the participants had peak-experiences. Such experiences provide meaning to life through the temporary transcendence of the diverse and conflicting elements of personality. Illustrative statements include "You just get a real good feeling . . . . I don't know what it is but it's just there after you start doing it " and "It makes me feel peaceful yet I think there's more to it. . . . really feeling good but I don't know how to explain it. It's hard to put into words but I like it."

An initial reflection on the results of this study is that they verify prior research on the effects of hatha yoga and meditation. The regular practice of these techniques significantly decreases anxiety, enhances body image and increases regard for self and others. However, the present study showed that a control group participating in highly similar activities to hatha yoga and meditation did not have similar effects on the same indices of psychophysical health. No prior studies reviewed by the author had compared hatha yoga and meditation to a similar technique. It may be that the vigorous physical exercises of volleyball, basketball and similar sports mainly affect the skeletal-muscular system and have minimum rehabilitative effects on the underlying psychophysiological systems. In contrast, hatha yoga and meditation, consisting of stable postures requiring mental focusing and little energy consumption, appears to have maximum rehabilitative effects on psychophysiology.

The potential applications of hatha yoga and meditation within education, medicine, and psychology are limited only by the lack of professionals in these areas who are also competent instructors of hatha yoga and meditation. Psychologist Seymour Fisher has already called for the use of psychophysiological techniques designed to enhance the body images of children.[20] His quite voluminous research into the area of body boundaries and body image has indicated that the development of body awareness by young people could prevent the later occurrence of psychiatric disorders. Cognitive efficiency in the face of distraction, the ability to tolerate a wide variety of stressful situations, better adjustment to injury, sickness and pregnancy and superior interpersonal behavior in groups are related to a positive body image. Hatha yoga and meditation could be of considerable value in elementary education if Fisher and Sidney Cleveland are correct in believing:

> . . . the manner which an individual meaningfully organizes body sensations becomes one of the primary dimensions in his overall system of standards for organizing the world.[21]

The education of the adolescent in our culture might be enhanced through the inclusion of hatha yoga and meditation in school curriculums. Adolescents are trying to establish their personal identity apart from parental expectations and demands and the failure to do so results in a diffuse and inadequate sense of self. The practice of hatha yoga and meditation, by tuning the adolescent into natural and enjoyable sensations of the body and a sense of mental control, could establish a sound sense of identity based upon the awareness of actual psychophysiological functioning. Also, as this study peripherally indicated, hatha yoga and meditation could prevent or replace the need for drug abuse as the adolescent finds a sense of meaning, power and pleasure residing within.

Within adult education hatha yoga and meditation could be used to teach the importance of inner sources of pleasure as opposed to the ultimately unfulfilling pursuit of symbolic pleasures such as wealth, status, physical attractiveness, and possessions. Such a reorientation toward inner sources of fulfillment and away from external sources of satisfaction is an essential task of the middle years of life.[22]

The applications of hatha yoga and meditation within medicine have been largely confined to the use of meditation in the treatment of hypertension and related heart disease and severe tension related syndromes such as migraine and tension headaches and temperomandibular jaw syndrome. Anxiety plays a clear role in the development of much disease and although not all disease is psychosomatic, the partial or complete recovery from a wide variety of acute and chronic diseases might be facilitated through hatha yoga and meditation. Perhaps the morbid fascination with the body by the hypochondriac could be reoriented toward a healthy concern and experience of the body through the techniques. It is clear that individuals practicing hatha yoga and meditation report the spontaneous relief or elimination of a *very* wide range of physical dysfunctions and further inquiry into this area could become a rather productive field of research.

It is clear that hatha yoga and meditation could serve as a powerful adjunct in the treatment of psychiatric syndromes in which the reduction of anxiety and/or depression played a prominent role in the focus of therapy. As there are no side-effects with hatha yoga and meditation, potent tranquilizers and anti-depressant drugs might be replaced in the management of symptoms.

A further psychological application of hatha yoga

and meditation is in the area of biofeedback training. In biofeedback training the individual is attempting to bring a psychophysiological function such as muscle tension or body temperature under conscious control and thereby correct dysfunctions such as tension or migraine headaches. The function is electronically monitored and the level of activity is amplified and made known immediately to the subject through auditory or visual signals. In this manner the amount of psychophysiological activity at any given moment can be controlled. Once the individual can control the original dysfunction through the biofeedback training, he/she could learn to maintain and even increase control independent of the electronic equipment through hatha yoga and meditation.

A final application of hatha yoga and meditation to be considered lies in the area of values. Humanistic psychologists seek to understand the deeper, innate values of our species through the process of self-actualization. Deficiency needs and defensive styles of being become uncovered as the individual consciously chooses to explore and identify with the transcendent self. The truth, goodness and beauty characterizing this higher self come to be directly perceived and thus illuminate all levels of personality. Hatha yoga and meditation is a method of quieting and controlling the body and mind, thereby facilitating the progress of self-actualization and the experience of these deeper values.

## References

1. Maslow, A. *Toward a Psychology of Being.* New York: D. Van Nostrand, 1968.
2. Jourard, S. *Healthy Personality: An Approach from the View-point of Humanistic Psychology.* New York: Macmillan Publishing Co., Inc., 1974.
3. Brar, H. "Yoga and Psychoanalysis" *British Journal of Psychiatry,* 1970, 116, 201-206.
4. Wolpe, J. *Psychotherapy by Reciprocal Inhibition.* Stanford, Conn.: Stanford University Press, 1958.
5. Shapiro, D., & Zifferblatt, S. "Zen Meditation and Behavioral Self Control: Similarities, Differences and Clinical Applications," *American Psychologist,* 1976, 31, 7, 519-532.
6. Benson, H. *The Relaxation Response.* New York: William Morrow and Company, 1975.
7. Udupa, K. & Singh, R. "The Scientific Basis of Yoga," *Journal of the American Medical Association.* 1972, 220, 1265.
8. Vahia, N., Vinekar, S., & Doongaji, D. "Some Ancient Indian Concepts in the Treatment of Psychiatric Disorders," *British Journal of Psychiatry,* 1966, 112, 1089-1096.
9. Benson, H., & Wallace, K. "Decreased Drug Use with Transcendental Meditation—A Study of 1,862 Subjects," in C. Zarafonetis (ed.), *Drug Abuse—Proceedings of the International Conference.* Philadelphia: Lea and Febiger, 1972.
10. Shaffi, M., Lavely, R. & Jaffee, R. "Meditation and Marijuana," *American Journal of Psychiatry,* 1974, 131, 60-63.
11. Ferguson, P., & Gowan, J. "The Influence of Transcendental Meditation on Anxiety, Depression, Aggression, Neuroticism and Self-Actualization," paper presented at the California State Psychological Association Convention, January, 1975.
12. Orme-Johnson, D. "Transcendental Meditation for Drug Abuse Counselors," in D. Orme-Johnson, L. Domash, & J. Farrow, (eds.), *Scientific Research on Transcendental Meditation: Collected Papers.* Los Angeles: M.I.U. Press, 1974.
13. Seeman, W., Nidich, S., & Banta, T. "The Influence of Transcendental Meditation on a Measure of Self-Actualization," *Journal of Counseling Psychology, 1972, 19, 184-187.*
14. Nidich, S., Seeman, W., & Dreskin, T. "Influence of Transcendental Meditation: A Replication," *Journal of Counseling Psychology,* 1973, 20, 555-556.
15. Blasdell, K. "The Effects of Transcendental Meditation upon a Complex Perceptual-Motor Task," in D. Orme-Johnson, L. Domash, & J. Farrow (eds.) *Scientific Research on Transcendental Meditation: Collected Papers.* Los Angeles: M.I.U. Press, 1974.
16. Graham, J. "Auditory Discrimination in Meditators," in D. Orme-Johnson, L. Domash, & J. Farrow (eds.) *Scientific Research on*

*Transcendental Meditation: Collected Papers.* Los Angeles: M.I.U. Press, 1974.

17. Linden, W. "Practicing of Meditation by School Children and Their Levels of Field Dependence—Independence, Test Anxiety, and Reading Achievement," *Journal of Consulting and Clinical Psychology*, 1973, 41, 1, 139-143.

18. Secord, P., & Jourard, S. "Body Size and Body Cathexis," *Journal of Consulting Psychology*, 1953, 17, 343-347.

19. Kurg, S., Scheier, I., & Cattell, R. *Handbook for the IPAT Anxiety Scale.* Champaign, Illinois: Institute for Personality and Ability Testing, 1976.

20. Fisher, S. *Body Consciousness: You Are What You Feel.* Englewood Cliffs, N.J.: Prentice-Hall, Inc., 1973.

21. Fisher, S., & Cleveland, S. *Body Image and Personality.* New York: Dover Publications, Inc., 1968.

22. Jung, C. *The Undiscovered Self.* Boston: Little, Brown and Company, 1958.

# Meditation and Biofeedback in the Regulation of Internal States

## JEAN KRISTELLER

Your heart is pounding. Your breath is shallow and irregular. You notice your hands are moist as you clench your fists and all your muscles feel tense. You try to bring yourself under control, becoming embarassed because someone might notice how upset you are. As you try harder to relax, you continue to feel your heart pound. You get angry at yourself for not being in control and feel even worse.

We have all experienced anxiety, fear and the feeling of being out of control. Are we at the mercy of these feelings, or can we learn to regulate our bodies, our minds and our emotions to transcend such experiences? These feelings are complex, involving many of the systems in ourselves: our physiological reactions, our thoughts, and how we act. Psychologists are far from fully understanding these systems or how they interact to engender feelings of anxiety in stressful situations. But the knowledge they are gaining through research is helping individuals to gain greater control over themselves. Researchers are finding that through growth of personal knowledge and self-regulation, whether by ancient techniques such as meditation, modern techniques like biofeedback, or some optimum combination, it is possible to regulate and reduce uncontrolled reactions to stress.

All of us have things we fear or become anxious about. Some fears are as simple and circumscribed as fears of spiders, or of snakes. We may be afraid of speaking up in front of others, afraid of being evaluated, or afraid of getting close to other people. Feelings of anxiety accompany such fears. Anxiety can be related to various objects or situations or be so intangible that we cannot express in words, either to other people or to ourselves, what it is that causes these feelings.

There is no single good way to measure anxiety. That is because anxiety is not a single entity. When we face a stressful situation, whether an airplane flight, a new job, or a confrontation with an old friend, and our reaction is to become 'anxious,' each of us reacts in many different ways. The activity of the autonomic nervous system changes, resulting in the reaction described above. Our thoughts replay similar situations from our past, and we may relive doubt, guilt, or shame which we experienced the last time we were in that situation. Behavior also varies greatly. Some people force themselves on the airplane and use a good stiff drink to cope with their anxiety. Others change their lives to avoid the stress, never going hiking in the woods, or not taking a job which involves meeting strangers. The latter is a very effective way to avoid the physical and emotional disturbances, but often backfires as the individual makes more and more changes to avoid anything which even reminds him/her of the original anxiety. Finally a rigid life style may develop, completely controlled by fear.

Three systems have just been described: physiological, cognitive and behavioral. By breaking down the experience of anxiety into disturbances in any or all of these three systems, psychologists are able to investigate, either for research or clinical purposes, the complexity of the phenomenon. It is important to consider that these three systems do not in their sum define anxiety. The physiological analysis is limited to looking at large changes in the autonomic nervous system, the EEG wave form, or in major organs. Cognitive analysis deals primarily with what can be verbally expressed. Behavioral analysis is concerned with what can be reliably recorded by an outside observer. There are also many aspects of the experience of anxiety which are difficult or impossible to express verbally, but which are acutely felt by the individual, or which exist at an unconscious level but which subtly affect behavior. Perhaps these aspects need to be considered as another equally important system, but until better measuring devices are developed by the psychologist, understanding and control of this fourth system may be largely delegated to the individual and/or to the 'spiritual' teacher.

These systems do not operate independently. In fact, it is very important to keep in mind that the distinctions above are made for the purpose of understanding something which is too complex to be researched, or frequently even treated, without looking at its components. The danger in looking at the systems separately is the tendency to revert to a philosophical position which tacitly accepts a fundamental difference between mind and body, the duality of being, which continues to plague Western medicine.

Science still has very far to go in understanding the process involved in each of these four systems; fortunately, many of the laboratories involved in this work are also looking at the interdependencies involved. How are these systems studied and measured? Most people have had some experience taking tests developed by psychologists. These may be measuring intelligence, creativity, personality 'traits' such as self-esteem or 'need for achievement,' and social attitudes. Until recently, this kind of 'paper-and-pencil' test has been the primary, and frequently, the only way in which psychologists have studied anxiety. These tests are very good for getting at what people say about themselves when they are anxious or trying to cope with stressful situations, but are limited in that they rely on memory, and a language representation of emotion and behavior. Neither is very accurate nor reliable. Within the last two decades, psychologists have begun to look more directly at behavior. This may be done either in the laboratory, such as measuring how close a snake phobic can come to a snake, or in naturalistic settings, as when an agoraphobic keeps track of the time spent outside the house. In addition to providing a way of measuring one of the components of anxiety, behavioral measures are reliably observable by more than one person, unlike thoughts or feelings, and are frequently trusted more as measures of change in anxiety over time.

The third system most frequently measured by psychologists is the physiological system. While people can be asked about how their heart rate is changing or if they feel 'tense,' people are often not very accurate about these changes; it is very difficult to pinpoint them in time; and subtle bodily reactions may go completely unnoticed. A number of diseases, such as hypertension (high blood pressure), ulcers, and asthma, have been recognized for a long time as being related to stress and to styles of coping with stress. However, by the time these develop fully, they may be relatively unrelated to current incidents. Most of what goes on in our bodies we are not aware of, unless something goes wrong. We are conscious of messages sent by the nerves in our skin and joints, in many of our muscles, and by our primary senses, though even the majority of these are merely background noise for the one or two signals to which we are paying careful attention. Most of the monitoring of the body systems which maintain a basic assumption of Western medicine posits that a homeostatic balance goes on completely unnoticed. In fact, it is impossible for us to notice most of the electrical and chemical signals at a conscious level because the proper nerve cells simply do not exist. While we can monitor when our stomach starts to churn, we cannot usually tell the state of our liver; the brain itself has no 'pain' nerves, allowing for brain surgery under a local scalp anaesthetic. This assumption is beginning to be re-examined as documented reports of such subtle control, by yogis and other individuals trained by Eastern techniques, reach the West.

Until technology was developed to measure these subtle changes in the autonomic nervous systems, much of the body was like a 'black box.' The standard equipment of the psychophysiologist who looks at how physiological and psychological systems of the human interact, is the polygraph, a multi-channel (poly) recorder (graph) of signals from the heart (EKG or ECG), the muscles (EMG), the sweat glands (SCL—skin conductance level), the brain (EEG) and of respiration. The EEG (electroencephalogram) measures activity in the central nervous system; the rest of the measures are from the peripheral, or autonomic, nervous system. The part of the autonomic system of most interest in the study of anxiety and stress is the sympathetic nervous system. When this is activated through complex signals from the brain, the organs involved for the most part increase their activity. The sympathetic nervous system prepares the body for emergencies and for muscular activity. The heart beats faster, muscles tense, sweat flows and breathing increases. Acting in opposition to this action but on the same organs is the parasympathetic nervous system, involved with restorative functions of rest and digestion. The activity of these nervous system networks creates changes in the very low level electrical fields which accompany the function of these various organs, and these small differences can be sensed by applying electrodes to the skin, then amplifying the signals via the polygraph, or sending them directly into a computer. By monitoring these signals, very subtle changes which accompany psychological events can be studied by the psychologist. More important to the discussion here is the extent to which this technology makes information about these physiological processes available at a conscious level to the individual whose heart rate or muscle tension is being monitored. This is the basis of biofeedback.

At this point we can return to the discussion of these systems in the context of learning how to control our anxiety under conditions of stress. Each of these systems are part of the whole of ourselves, but they do not all act in unison. Verbal report of feelings of anxiety do not always coordinate well with arousal in the sympathetic nervous system. People frequently force themselves to act in ways which appear calm and collected to the outside observer, while they feel very shaky inside. A person might also spend a lot of energy arranging his or her life so that very few stresses ever occur, but feel very uncertain of any inner unity or healthfulness which could sustain them under other circumstances.

By understanding the complexity of our reactions to stress, it becomes clearer why anxiety is a chronic problem for so many people and why an integrative approach to treatment is much more likely to be effective than an approach which limits itself to single symptoms. However, the ways in which these systems interact are very complex. While the final goal is to understand these interactions and use this understanding to support integrative approaches which help teach self-regulation under stress, the initial steps involve understanding the systems at a more basic level. One of the least understood factors in this total system is the physiological component. Until the last decade, most physicians and psychologists thought that it was not possible for people to learn to control most of the activity of the heart, or brain waves, or low level muscle activity. Several things came together to change this. As mentioned above, the technology to measure these systems accurately had been developed. Psychologists were interested in learning how to control in other ways, using what is called operant conditioning, which pairs successful attempts at a new task with some type of reward or reinforcement. A third important impetus was the appearance of reports in Western psychological journals of work being done in India, where researchers were monitoring the physiological functions of yogis who had developed such control through their practices. A new area, the learned control of physiological functions, grew slowly over a few years and became what is now known as 'biofeedback.'

What is research in this area teaching us about control of these systems? Two of the systems which have been most intensively studied are the muscles and the heart. Biofeedback from the muscles is used to decrease activity when relaxation is the desired outcome, and is used to increase activity in damaged or atrophied muscles. It seems to function in a very similar way to the natural feedback of information from muscles which goes on all the time. Heart rate is more interesting because it is not normally under our direct control in the same way that the muscles in our arms or legs or forehead are, and yet change in heart rate is a sensitive indicator of stress and anxiety. A large number of studies demonstrated that by using biofeedback of heart rate, people could learn to control their heart, even when they were relaxed. Many of these studies showed controlled increases of about 10 beats per minute, but the decreases in rate were much smaller, if they were found at all. This was disappointing because the clinical effect desired was a decrease of heart rate. It was also puzzling at a theoretical level. If biofeedback was a single process, why wasn't it as easy to lower heart rate as to raise it, especially when people were relaxing the muscle activity which often accompanies increases? A series of studies run in the Department of Psychology at the University of Wisconsin, under the direction of Dr. Peter Lang, was designed to respond to this problem. Earlier studies in this laboratory had shown that learning to control increases in heart rate followed a 'motor skills' model. In other words, better control was found when people received more information about their heart rate and how they were doing, and when they were more highly motivated, for example, by paying people according to the amount of increase. Level of motivation and amount of information have been found to be important when people are trying to learn new motor skills. However, when people were being trained to lower their heart rate, these factors didn't seem to help.

Because this laboratory is associated with a psychology clinic, there is a lot of interest in treating problems such as anxiety and learned fear, and much of the research energy is spent on understanding the physiological changes which accompany effective treatment of these problems. We had looked at relaxation training, and biofeedback of muscle tension levels, but these did not seem to be more effective for training people to reduce their heart rate than did the heart rate biofeedback. We wondered if perhaps there was something intrinsic to biofeedback which interacted with the normal functioning of the cardiovascular system to prevent large decreases from appearing. It could be that the large amount of information that needs to be processed when an individual is paying attention to every heart beat keeps the system aroused to a point which counteracts the slowing. The alternative was to find a completely different training strategy, one that was also directed toward training self-regulation, but which involved a different process.

Many studies have been done which show that during meditation a number of the body processes slow down to a lower level of arousal and remain stable at these levels. However, these studies had not directed the meditators to focus their attention on a single system, such as heart rate. We wondered if meditation, as it involves no processing of external information, might be a more effective training technique to lower heart rate than biofeedback, if the individual were to identify heart rate slowing as a desired outcome.

Because we wanted to start with people who had had no previous training in meditation, and because our eventual goal is to develop training methods to help people who come into a clinic, we decided to use a simple meditation task developed by Dr. Herbert Benson to study meditation in the laboratory. He has shown that the physiological changes which accompany practice of this technique were very similar to those found in people practicing Transcendental Meditation. The technique, if compared to the highly developed and refined methods of traditional meditation practices such as Yoga meditation, might be better considered a pre-meditation training method. However, there are several important similarities which distinguish it from simple relaxation. The subjects in these studies were asked to relax their bodies, passively watch their breath while focusing their attention on thinking the word 'one' to themselves on each exhalation, and to passively let go of any thoughts which might intrude, as they noticed them. They were at no point informed that there were learning a meditation exercise. Subjects in the study came to three sessions. The first two were training sessions which alternated three minute slowing trials with one minute rest periods. Biofeedback subjects received feedback of their heart rate on a monitor during the first slowing trial. The next slowing trial was a 'transfer' trial. The subject closed his eyes and tried to transfer knowledge gained about his heart during the first trial to slow his heart unassisted by biofeedback equipment during the second trial. These two types of trials alternated five times in each training session. Meditation subjects practiced the same meditation exercise for every trial. Session three was a 15 minute 'transfer' period, during which the subjects were told to lower their heart rate as much as possible, using the control developed during the first two sessions.

We were also interested in how variations in information and motivation would effect control of heart rate decrease for the meditation subjects. If the motor skills model were correct, then we would expect the meditators who were in the low motivation group and who received no additional information about their heart rate to perform the poorest. Subjects who were to receive additional information saw a summary of their heart rate at the end of each transfer trial. Instead of using money to vary level of motivation, we decided to separate the subjects into two groups, an 'experimental treatment' group and a 'clinical treatment' group. A common criticism of laboratory research is that it may not be applicable to a clinical setting because experimenters are too business-like and cold, and do not interact with the subjects as a therapist would, or give personalized information as to how 'treatment' is going. We treated half the subjects as a high involvement group and the other half as a low involvement group. The low involvement subjects had little personal contact with the experimenter and had no opportunity to get additional knowledge about the training tasks or their use of these tasks. The high involvement group, on the other hand, received a mimeograph sheet discussing either biofeedback or meditation; they were encouraged to ask questions and were cautioned if they started using inappropriate breathing patterns; after each session the experimenter discussed their progress with them and they were encouraged to practice at home.

Our results confirmed our idea that control of heart rate slowing was a very different process from heart rate speeding. In three separate studies, involving over 100 people, the meditation subjects slowed their heart rate more than did the biofeedback subjects. This difference was statistically significant in the first and last study. Furthermore, in the last study in which motivation and information level were also manipulated, we had some very interesting results. Contrary to what we expected, the meditation subjects who received no additional information and who were in the low involvement group slowed their heart rate the most, with the average amount being about 9 beats per minute. In fact, by the third session the meditation subjects who were 'highly involved' were doing no better than the feedback subjects. The advantages which the more passive, inner-directed meditation task had over biofeedback were negated when the subjects were encouraged to become more highly goal oriented and were made more aware of their progress. The effect of goal orientation is certainly not simple. The studies of Transcendental Meditation done by Robert Wallace and Herbert Benson showed decreases in heart rate of between 3 and 5 beats per minute. Using a similar meditation exercise, when we directed attention to heart rate slowing as the goal of the task, we found decreases averaging 9 beats per minute. However, when we sought to make this goal more salient for our subjects, the heart rate decreases were no different from those of our biofeedback subjects, and were similar to those obtained by Wallace and Benson. This distinction between two degrees of task or goal orientation bears some relevance to the actual practice of meditation over extended periods of time. The extent to which one is goal oriented during meditation practice is often a difficult problem for beginning meditators. Most individuals begin the practice of meditation because they wish to make some changes in their life. Yet it is emphasized by teachers of meditation that it is important to not be goal oriented, because that active seeking is counter to the very process of change occuring in meditation. While we identified heart rate slowing as the task, the focus for the low involvement subjects was kept more directed to the meditation exercise itself, than was the focus for the high involvement subjects.

Dr. Elmer Green at the Menninger Institute has developed the concept of passive volition in discussing the process of learning effective control of physiological functions during biofeedback. He considers that the main factor related to successful control is the immediate knowledge of the state of the physiological system, possible via biofeedback. Our data demonstrates that this does not seem to be the case for slowing heart rate, at least if training is limited to three or four sessions. However, Green's premise is that the biofeedback is important not so much in and of itself, but because it makes it easier for the individual to learn to produce autonomic passivity, or 'passive volition.' Green has described how migraine patients being trained to raise peripheral temperature may struggle actively to produce these changes to no avail and are successful 'give up' and become detached from the task. This experience of watchful detachment, rather than the active volition we usually associate with learning a new skill, is also characteristic of successful meditation. Anxiety also involves a type of active 'holding on,' a negative preoccupation with the feared object, whether it be a snake or the thought of 'looking foolish.' Meditation involves a 'letting go,' of being comfortable with challenges and satisfied with old memories, not dwelling on them, but living in the present instead. The mechanisms by which this happens are still largely inaccessible, especially to the Western scientist who lacks personal knowledge of the processes involved.

In the present study, it appears that use of a meditation exercise, when accompanied by the proper state of mind, is more helpful in producing certain physiological changes which are opposite those seen during states of stress and anxiety, than is biofeedback alone. The study certainly needs to be extended by research which looks at the treatment of people actually seeking relief from anxiety, but our results do support the idea that the practice of meditation has great potential for establishing a state of being which allows healthy changes to take place in the direction of increased self-regulation.

# Yoga and Biofeedback: A Treatment Program

PHIL NUERNBERGER, Ph.D.

Health professionals are becoming increasingly aware of the powerful effect mental events and patterns have on our physical well-being. A significant degree of the health problems we suffer in our society are increasingly recognized as having their origins and continuance in the mind. In other words, our conscious and unconscious mental/emotional patterns often lead to harmful physiological changes. It has only been recently discovered by Western science that we have the ability to consciously alter physiological functions which were previously thought to be automatic and uncontrollable responses. Such physiological responses as neuron firings in muscles, vascular dilation or contraction, heartbeats and blood pressure to name just a few, have all been shown to be amenable to conscious manipulation and at least some conscious control over the autonomic system for the past 4,000 years and has extensive knowledge in this area, which is so new to Western science. One of the consequences of this new understanding in the West is the process called biofeedback.

Biofeedback is the term given to the process in which some physiological response is monitored by sensitive equipment, converted into a recognizable signal, and provided to the subject. In this manner the subject gains conscious knowledge of the ongoing physiological process which previously was unavailable to his/her awareness. Biofeedback treatment is the application of this process to gain conscious control over those physiological activities which are involved in psychosomatic dysfunction. Biofeedback by itself is a simple informational process which is not clinically useful unless it is part of a comprehensive program in the development of inner awareness and thus conscious control over these physiological processes. Often biofeedback is used as a straight conditioning process in which the subject is rewarded for controlling the signal. Recent studies have shown this conditioning process to be of very little clinical usefulness, as the ability to control the underlying physiological process is lost when the biofeedback equipment is no longer available to the subject.

It is important to realize that biofeedback is a useful therapeutic tool when used as part of a holistic program in which the goal is to gain control over physiological processes through increased conscious awareness of those physiological processes *and* the mental/emotional events which precede the physiological changes.  For the past three years, we have been developing a therapeutic approach to psychosomatic dysfunction based on increasing self awareness.  The focus of the program has been on the development of practical clinical tools based on yoga science.  This work has been done in the Biofeedback Treatment Program of the Minneapolis Clinic of Psychiatry and Neurology.  What has evolved over the past three years is a very effective and efficient treatment program relying on yoga science in conjunction with biofeedback and brief psychotherapy.

The training program is based on a systematic approach.  In the first interview, which generally lasts an hour, the patients talk about their presenting problem and how it affects their lifestyle.  They are taken through a beginning muscle relaxation exercise, which is recorded on a cassette tape for practice at home.  Diaphragmatic breathing is also taught and an introductory session on the EMG biofeedback machine is provided.  The patient is to practice the diaphragmatic breathing and the relaxation exercise at least twice daily.  In the second session, the patient is generally taught some basic yoga joint and gland exercises to supplement the relaxation, breathing and concentration exercises.  The following week a yogic breathing/relaxation exercise is taped for the patient along with an introductory meditation exercise using *mantra*.  Subsequent sessions practice on the biofeedback machines along with discussion of the kinds of problems the patient faces in his/her everyday life. Psychotherapy is as brief and direct as possible, geared toward developing conscious awareness of non-helpful emotional/mental/behavioral patterns. Based on individual need, other yogic breathing and "cleansing" exercises are also taught.

In order to present an idea of the scope and success of this treatment program, a brief summary of the patient characteristics and their success rates and the results of a long-term follow-up survey will be presented first. An in-depth discussion of the principles and techniques used in the program will follow.

In 1975, 106 patients, most of whom had suffered from chronic psychosomatic symptoms over several years, completed the yoga-biofeedback program. Patient improvement was rated by both the therapist and patient on the basis of decreased pain intensity, pain frequency, felt anxiety, usage of medication, and increased ability to sleep and sense of well-being.

Table I presents the diagnostic categories and the number of patients successfully and unsuccessfully treated. The two largest diagnostic categories were headaches and phobic anxiety. As shown in the table, 50 of 56 (89%) of the headache patients and 25 of 26 (96.2%) of the phobic anxiety patients were rated as improved upon termination from the program. This is not surprising in that termination was based on the decrease of symptoms and medication, and was a mutual decision of the therapist and patient. However, what is surprising was that length of treatment averaged only 5.34 weekly sessions.

## TABLE I

Diagnostic Categories, Improvement Rates and the Number of Patients
Referred to the Biofeedback Treatment Program

| Diagnostic Category | Improved | | Failed to Improve | | Totals | Drop-outs |
|---|---|---|---|---|---|---|
| | No. | % | No. | % | No. | No. |
| Headaches | 50 | 89.3 | 6 | 10.7 | 56 | 17 |
| Tension 27 | | | | | | |
| Migraine 3 | | | | | | |
| Tension-migraine 20 | | | | | | |
| Anxiety | 25 | 96.2 | 1 | 3.8 | 26 | 7 |
| Other* | 11 | 45.8 | 13 | 54.2 | 24 | 11 |
| Totals | 86 | 81.1 | 20 | 18.9 | 106 | 35 |
| Average Number of Sessions | 5.34 | | 5.71 | | | 1.74 |

* Includes: essential hypertension, Spasmotic Tarticollus (wry neck), low
back pain and Reynards Disease.

## TABLE II

Male and Female Comparisons

| | Improved | Failed to Improve | Drop-outs |
|---|---|---|---|
| Males | 32 | 11 | 12 |
| Females | 54 | 9 | 23 |

A total of 35 patients dropped out of the treatment program without completing the training. As shown in Table I, the average number of sessions for those who dropped was 1.74. The average number of sessions for the twenty patients who remained in the program but who *failed* to show improvement was 5.71. As mentioned above, those who were treated successfully averaged only 5.34 sessions. Of these, the average number of sessions in which the successfully treated patient received actual biofeedback was 3.52 sessions.

As one can see by the results, by the fifth session, the patient and therapist were usually fairly certain that the presenting symptomology had undergone significant changes. Headaches were under control; that is, the frequency and intensity of the pain had considerably lessened. Also the feelings and symptoms of anxiety, such as hyperventilation, chest pain, insomnia, apprehension, etc., had been significantly relieved. No attempt was made to achieve any particular level of ability *vis a vis* the biofeedback levels. That is, there was no pre-set level of muscle tension or skin temperature that was used as a goal. The primary goals were symptom relief and the patient's confidence and skill in relaxation, concentration and breathing techniques, and in an increased self-awareness. A major focus was on developing the patient's ability to continue developing his/her skills of self-observation and inner-awareness and inner-calm.

In order to gauge the long-term effectiveness of the treatment program, a 17 question follow-up survey was completed in which attempts were made to contact by phone all of the 86 successfully treated patients who lived in the Minneapolis-St. Paul area. A minimum of three calls were made to reach each patient. A total of 40 patients were contacted in this manner and were interviewed over the phone. The following chart shows the number and percentage of successfully treated patients who were contacted. The average time span between termination from the program and being interviewed for the follow-up survey was one year, with a range of 6.75 months to 19.25 months.

## TABLE III

Follow Up Sample

|  | Headaches | Anxiety | Other | Total |
|---|---|---|---|---|
| Number of improved patients, 1975 | 50 | 25 | 11 | 86 |
| Number of patients in follow-up | 24 | 13 | 3 | 40 |
| Percent of follow-up to total | 48% | 52% | 27% | 46.5% |

The patients were asked to rate the present condition of their problem, their present state of well-being, whether or not they had returned to a physician for further treatment, and how they evaluated the treatment program. They were also asked to respond to nine of the 17 items on a scale of 1 to 7. Table IV presents a summary of the mean (average) responses to these nine questions.

The responses to the survey were overwhelmingly favorable. As shown in Table IV, patients indicated

## TABLE  IV

### Average Ratings of Nine Items from the Follow-up Survey Questionnaire

| QUESTIONNAIRE ITEM | AVERAGE OF RATINGS | | |
| --- | --- | --- | --- |
| | Headache<br>N=24 | Anxiety<br>N=13 | Total<br>N=40 |
| 1. Rate the present condition of your problem.<br>1 (worse) to 7 (completely gone) | 5.7 | 5.8 | 5.7 |
| 2. How helpful would you rate the therapy program<br>1 (not helpful) to 7 (very helpful) | 5.8 | 6.1 | 5.8 |
| 3. Rate the intensity of your pain or tension.<br>1 (severe) to 7 (none) | 5.4 | 5.9 | 5.6 |
| 4. Rate the frequency of your pain or tension.<br>1 (severe) to 7 (none) | 5.7 | 5.5 | 5.5 |
| 5. Rate changes in the amount of medication since biofeedback training.<br>1 (greatly increased) to 7 (greatly decreased) | 6.1 | 5.6 | 6.1 |
| 6. Rate your ability to sleep since yoga-biofeedback training.<br>1 (decreased ability) to 7 (increased ability) | 6.1 | 6.2 | 6.1 |
| 7. Rate your sense of well-being since yoga-biofeedback training (how content, etc.).<br>1 (greatly decreased) to 7 (greatly increased) | 5.6 | 6.4 | 5.9 |
| 8. Rate how often others (family, friends, co-workers) have commented on changes in you.<br>1 (many negative responses) to 7 (many positive responses) | 5.9 | 6.1 | 6.0 |
| 9. Compare yoga-biofeedback training with other kinds of treatments you undertook.<br>1 (least helpful) to 7 (most helpful) | 6.0 | 6.3 | 6.1 |

Four was used as the center response indicating "no change" or "no difference."

continued decrease in pain frequency and intensity, and a continued decrease in amount of medication used. They also reported an increased sense of well-being and an increased ability to sleep. Furthermore, they indicated that other individuals remarked positively about their behavior and improvement. The tone of the remarks indicated that the "significant others" felt that the patients were happier and easier to get along with. The patients also rated the yoga-biofeedback program as being helpful, and in fact, more helpful than other modes of treatment (unspecified) than they had undertaken in order to solve their problem.

Only two patients (5% of follow-up sample) reported "no change" or a worsened condition. These two patients were also the only ones who reported that they no longer practiced their relaxation, concentration and breathing exercises! Only nine patients (22.5%) of follow-up sample) returned to a physician for further treatment of the original problem.

Fully 37 of the 40 patients (92.5%) reported that they still practiced the relaxation and/or breathing and/or concentration exercises taught in the program. Eighteen of these patients still practiced at least once daily.

All 40 of the patients in the follow-up sample reported that they would recommend the treatment program to others. When asked what they considered to be the most useful part of the treatment program the following responses were given:

9 (22.5%) biofeedback most important

8 (20%) relaxation/meditation tapes the most important

8 (20%) relationship with the therapist most important

15 (38.5%) a combination of the above

Although the termination data and the follow-up data were not collected in a strict scientific manner, the results certainly indicate that the therapy program is an effective and efficient treatment of the psychosomatic dysfunctions of chronic headaches and chronic anxiety. Most of the patients, particularly the headache patients, had suffered from their problems for periods of 10 to 15 years or longer without any significant relief. Now, within a five to six week period, they were experiencing significant periods of relief *without* the use of drugs. Most often, the patients described significant improvement in a wide variety of areas in their life. Patients frequently told of significant changes in how they perceived their immediate environments, particularly they reported increased closeness to loved ones, less hostility, and felt less burdensome responsibility for others' emotional states. Several patients reported increased feelings of personal freedom.

### Principles and Techniques

The success of the therapy program is the result of a holistic approach to psychosomatic dysfunction. That is, the symptoms that bring the patient to the therapy program are seen in context of the individual's unique perceptual/emotional/behavioral response to life. This holistic approach derives its fundamental structure from yoga science and philosophy and utilizes practical yoga exercises which lead to mental and physical well-being.

The significant causal factor in psychosomatic dysfunction, indeed, in most of the major health problems in our Western culture, is a sustained state of stress in the individual. Much has already been written about our "pressure cooker" technological society with its attendant anxieties, ulcers, heart attacks, over-worked executives, highly competitive educational and financial institutions, etc. By now we recognize that it is a truism to talk about the high degree of stress and/or tension manifest in our society. We are also beginning to recognize that the direct results of this stress are numerous physical and mental disabilities, ranging from cardiac problems to drug addiction, including the two problems which are prominent in the therapy program, chronic headaches and chronic phobic anxiety. However, we fail to recognize that the individual is responsible for the creation of these dysfunctions, and can assume responsibility for alleviating the dysfunction.

Traditional medical treatment for psychosomatic dysfunction (other than radical surgery), has generally taken two directions, both of which have been fairly ineffectual in curing the dysfunctions. The primary medical approach is to treat the symptom, e.g., head pain, by the use of a wide variety of drugs. The intent is symptomatic relief, with little effort made to alter the causal factor of stress. Pain killers to mask pain, tranquilizers to reduce anxiety, muscle relaxants to reduce muscle tension are all widely prescribed to a williing public. This pharmacological approach is significant in its failure to cure psychosomatic dysfunction. Even when successfully and properly used, drugs provide largely temporary symptomatic relief, and not substantive *cure*. However the drugs often produce side effects, sometimes more negative than the original problem. Furthermore many patients become addicted to their medications. Related to this pharmacological approach are the millions of dollars spent each year on over-the-counter drugs which scientific evidence shows are almost completely ineffectual.

The secondary medical approach involves some type of psychotherapeutic approach, either therapy groups, psychoanalysis, behavior modification, or some other form of "talking therapy." While a case can be made that this secondary approach is at least less destructive than the drug approach, and does at least recognize the rope of mental or life-style patterns in the etiology of the dysfunction, only very modest success can be shown.

The Biofeedback Treatment Program with yoga as its fundamental basis provides a direct treatment approach to both the stress and to the origin of the stress. Yoga recognizes that tension and/or stress and/or anxiety exists not in the environment, but is a consequence of the individual's perceptual/emotional/behavioral habits. That is, stress is created by how the individual perceives his or her relationship to the environment, and does not lie in the environment itself. According to yoga, the source of our pain lies in our ignorance; that is, in our *lack of awareness.* This lack of awareness permeates our entire existence, from the most mundane habits of everyday living to the most profound levels of consciousness. On a very practical level, we create and sustain pain and suffering by being unaware of the perceptual/emotional habits which result in a chronic state of tension. Often we are even unaware of the tension itself. Being accustomed to our habitual tension, we often do not recognize when this tension is increasing or decreasing. As long as we remain unaware (unconscious) of the patterns which result in stress and anxiety, we continue to generate and sustain the stress and anxiety. We then, of course, continue to suffer the consequences of this sustained stress, such as the psychosomatic dysfunctions of chronic head pain or chronic phobic anxiety.

Of course, the primary goal of the therapy program is to alleviate the symptomatic pain of chronic headaches or phobic anxiety, but to do so in such a fashion as to eliminate the conditions which lead to the dysfunction. Rather than focus on symptomatic relief (as done in the pharmacological approach) or behavioral or attitude change (as done in the "mental" or "behavioral" approach), the emphasis is on the expansion of conscious awareness of one's being in the world. As the individual increases his awareness of himself, he chooses more appropriate responses to the environment, becoming more self-confident and less fearful and defensive, and thus reduces the stress involved in living.  By being aware of physical and mental stress, and to the perceptual/emotional patterns that result in stress and/or anxiety, the individual is able to more quickly reduce the stress, and more importantly, to *avoid creating* the stress in the first place.

Although each patient is unique, and treatment is tailored to that uniqueness, there are several constancies to the therapy program.   The first step is to teach the patient to control the relaxation response;  that is, to be able to effectively and efficiently reduce physical tension through training the concentration powers of the mind.   Yogic relaxation, concentration and meditation exercises are taped for each patient. The patients practice these exercises at least twice daily for 20 to 25 minutes. The key to yogic exercises is the concentration on, and control of, the breath.  In fact, breath is so important that all patients are taught diaphragmatic breathing in the first session.

Although there are a variety of useful relaxation exercises which are utilized, concentration on and control of the breathing process leads directly to control of the emotional states.  While Western medicine and psychology talk about the relationship between mind and body, there is no definition or knowledge of what that relationship is. Yoga science defines that relationship as the breathing process.  In the therapy program, the simple technique of breath awareness is the tool which facilitates the expansion of awareness. Breathing exercises and breath awareness are central to the therapy program.

Biofeedback is also utilized to increase the individual's inner awareness processes. Rather than being used as a conditioning process where the emphasis is on controlling the biofeedback signal, the biofeedback is used as an informational tool. The patient is asked to pay attention to the inner thoughts, feelings and movements which are occurring in relationship to the biofeedback signal. A variety of biofeedback tools are used in the therapy program: EMG (muscle feedback), skin temperature, Palmer Conductance, EEG (brain waves) and pulse feedback. The primary feedback tool is the EMG (muscle tension) feedback, with temperature training the second most used feedback system. The biofeedback training is an important part of training the relaxation response and in teaching patients how to observe inner experiences, but it is only part of the holistic approach developed in the therapy program.

A variety of other tools are frequently used. Joints and glands exercises, derived from yoga, particularly the neck and shoulder rolls, are extremely useful in reducing muscle tension and developing bodily awareness. Patients are often referred to qualified hatha yoga instructors to continue developing awareness and control. Another useful tool has been the nasal wash, particularly for headache patients where there is some nasal or sinus involvement.

Psychotherapy is another major tool of the therapy

program.  Yoga provides the fundamental principles and direction of the psychotherapy.  Yoga psychology clearly shows that our suffering is a result of a lack of awareness of our true Be-ing.  In other words, we identify ourselves with transient emotional states and personality patterns which lead up and down and all around, with no center of stability.  The process of yoga therapy is one of dis-identifying with the personality or ego in order that we may clearly understand, and thus control, our personality.

Yoga therapy is geared towards *objective neutral observation* of the personality by the Self, or Consciousness, in order that the dynamic causal motivations can be made conscious, i.e., brought to conscious awareness. Patients are taught how to "dis-identify" with the feeling state.  When there is identification with the emotion, e.g., "I am lonely" rather than "I am experiencing a *feeling* of loneliness," than direct perceptual knowledge of the underlying motivational patterns will not be available to the person.  His/her attention is caught by the emotion and goes on the up and down joyride of the mood swings.  There is no constant, no still or quiet center of identity from which to observe the on-going mental/emotional patterns.

Learning to dis-identify oneself from emotional ups and downs allows one to begin to consciously be aware of the subtle choices he/she is making. When one becomes aware of choosing particular responses and the consequences of those choices, he becomes more free to choose responses which are more useful and satisfying.

This process of choice is a result of neutral observation. To develop this ability requires the practice of both *active* or *concentrative* meditation (sitting quietly and bringing the mind to one-pointed concentration) and *passive* meditation, often called *meditation in action.* Passive meditation is the art of being in a state of neutral observation throughout the entire day. The immediate consequence of this state of awareness is a reduction of the personal involvement in defensive or fearful or overemotional reactions.

A variety of techniques are used to help the patient increase his ability to be more aware of themselves, including breath awareness, breathing and meditation exercises and neutralizer words (the use of language to avoid judgmental processes). A non-judgmental acceptance is consciously communicated to the patient in order to help him/her develop this attitude towards him/herself. An alert experimental feeling toward the personality is gradually developed in the therapy process. This is a result of an increased awareness brought about by the consistent practice of meditation. As patients develop their ability to  meditate, they receive greater benefits from the other tools in the therapy program.

By and large the Yoga-Biofeedback Treatment Program has been very successful. As we learn more about applying yogic principles and techniques to direct therapy situations, we hope to expand and improve the program further. All human beings are in a process of natural growth and expansion. The therapy program is geared toward allowing that natural process to occur by facilitating the expansion of the conscious mind toward the state of Pure Consciousness.

# Holistic Therapy

RUDOLPH M. BALLENTINE, JR., M.D.

Mrs. A. had been suffering with a hyper-
active and enlarged thyroid gland for two
years. It had been treated with a medication
which suppressed thyroid activity but she
continued to feel tired, unhappy and not
well. The medication was working only
poorly. She came to the Himalayan Institute
and entered the Combined Therapy Program
because the choices she was offered were
surgery and radiation treatment. Yet she
insisted that she *knew* (and that the endo-
crinologist had admitted) that there was
something causing her thyroid to be hyper-
active and "that they haven't discovered
what." She felt removing part of the thyroid
surgically or destroying part of it with radiation was only a superficial answer to her

problem.  She wanted to get to the bottom of it.

During her ten-day intensive program she began to recall "definite sensations" in the thyroid gland that she had had many times during arguments with her husband.  She felt sure that tenseness in the thyroid gland was more noticeable at times when she was upset or angry about something and didn't say what she wanted to say.  In biofeedback training she learned through the help of the feedback machine to decrease the tension in her neck and throat area.  During one such session, when the neck was relaxed, she burst into tears because of noises in the adjoining room. They brought to mind, during the time her neck and throat were relaxed, memories of wanting to scream out at her husband "because of his inconsiderate nature."    By concentrating on her breathing through techniques that she was learning in the program, she was able to remain calm in the face of these memories and gradually things began to fall into place for her.

Eventually she broke into uncontrollable tears while dealing with one of the older physicians on the staff and a homeopathic remedy taken at that time seemed to catalyze her realization that this encounter was similar to confrontations she had had with her father as a child. In fact, she felt "I was a child at that moment," but after this realization something clicked and her ability to "let go" of the tension in her thyroid and neck increased. From that point on she felt that her thyroid gland was softer and she began to feel calmer and more relaxed.

Over the months that followed she continued to improve and ultimately reported that she had worked out problems with her husband and had regained her normal energy, feeling as though "I have finally recovered my health." Meanwhile the thyroid had decreased markedly in size and symptoms of hyperactivity had faded away.

The patient's treatment included not only biofeedback and breathing training but also physical exercises and a very carefully tailored diet. Trace mineral analysis and supplementation also seemed to play an important role, as did the use of homeopathic remedies. But the landmarks along her road to recovery were mental events—insights and realizations.

Is it possible that a "purely medical disease" like hyperthyroidism is somehow related to what goes on in the mind? In the context of conventional medicine and psychology such an idea seems almost radical, as though one were carrying a favorite idea to extreme. Yet the perspective of the medical community is changing.  It is now fashionable to say that sixty to seventy per cent of all medical problems are "psychosomatic."  In other words, the mind plays a significant role in their development.  But if the mind can cause the development of a "psychosomatic" illness, does it not have the capacity to reverse it?  In a recent weekend held at the Himalayan Institute on biofeedback, Dr. Barbara Brown was a guest lecturer.  During informal conversations we had the opportunity to find out from her the sort of things that held her interest—what was personally exciting and engrossing for her.  She confided that her research in biofeedback had led her to a conclusion that she felt was nothing short of revolutionary:  *the mind can control the body*.  Of course we all know that the mind controls the body in many ways.  We know that if we decide to do so, our mind can cause our arm to rise or our foot to lift.  What she was talking about, however, was control of the body in subtler and less obvious ways than those to which we are accustomed to thinking.  What she meant, we discovered as we talked, was that the mind has the power to control the body, not just in its voluntary functions but in its involuntary ones as well, that, in fact, the mind has the power to control the body *completely* in *any* of its aspects.

It is biofeedback which has done the most, probably, to change the perspective of the professional community in America.  Through the work of such pioneers as Dr. Barbara Brown, it has gradually become evident that certain physiological processes can be retrained, eliminating the basis for many diseases. If, indeed, the mind learns somehow to mismanage the body, why should it not be able to *re*learn, to correct this mismanagement and to regulate the body properly? In fact, research in biofeedback has shown repeatedly that patients who have tension headaches can learn through the use of the feedback device to reduce the tension much below the level they normally considered "relaxed." Once they become aware of the tension that they did not before recognize and learn how to eliminate it the tension headaches are virtually eradicated.

While the idea that the mind can control the body in a nearly unlimited way is a startling discovery for the contemporary medical community, it is nothing new to the practitioner of yoga. In fact, it has been the stock in trade of the yoga masters for millenia and a thorough understanding of all the implications of this notion that the mind can control the body and a diligent application of it account for many of the "inexplicable" feats performed by yogis both now and in the past.

But to what length can this idea be carried? If the mind has such potential for controlling the body, why need one suffer from diseases? To explore the possibilities and potentialities for therapy we set up at the Himalayan Institute an innovative program designed to provide one with an intensive reorientation toward his body, his emotions, his mind and their maintenance in a healthy state. Inspired by the teachings of yoga, we reasoned that the roots of disease could be found in bad habits, not merely bad habits in the sense of the use of cigarettes, alcohol or "junk foods," but bad habits that operate outside our usual field of awareness;  subtler habits; habits that have to do with our way of using the internal organs, with our way of positioning our bodies, with our way of holding tension in certain areas, with our way of breathing, for example.  If one could open his awareness to these subtle habits, if he could become alerted to how he was misusing his body, might he not gradually reshape his habits in such a way as to contribute to health rather than destroying it?

Yet habits have a momentum of their own.  To break this momentum is not an easy matter.  Ordinarily one's life habits, social contacts, schedule, work, etc., are inadvertently engineered to maintain him in the habits he has set up for himself.  As one evolves such a "life-style" the patterns he establishes are self-perpetuating and one habit is elaborated to cover up the effects of another so that the whole complex has a self-sustaining organization of its own.

But what if we removed the average person from his customary environment?  What if we deliberately set him down in a different kind of "culture"?  What if we eliminated his usual social reenforcements, his interpersonal patterns that sustained him in his "habit life"?  What if this were coupled with intensive training in relaxation and breathing, an introduction to the process of meditation, by training and turning the attention inwards, becoming aware of what bubbles up from the innermost reaches of the mind? If it were not possible to continue one's habits, would not their roots begin to show? If one were learning simultaneously methods of maintaining calmness and inner awareness, might he not be able to come to terms with the roots of these habits, roots which before were both inaccessible and intolerable?

Actually the Combined Therapy Program was not set up quite so deliberately as the above reasoning might imply. In fact, it seemed to evolve almost on its own. Biofeedback had been a part of the Institute program since its early days. It was during the period when biofeedback research was pioneered at the Menninger Clinic that Swami Rama was in residence there. His teachings and example did much to stimulate an awareness of the potentiality for self-regulation and after his departure the research team visited India to study other practitioners of yoga. The ultimate outcome of this expedition was a film entitled "Biofeedback—The Yoga of the West." Meanwhile when Swami Rama began to establish the Himalayan Institute in Chicago, he brought with him biofeedback technology as a practical, understandable and scientific link between modern medical science and the ancient practices of yoga. Both physicians and patients could appreciate the simplicity and practicality of relearning to use the body, of learning to eliminate tension or relax muscles.

Moreover, biofeedback serves another purpose. For many people it is a first encounter with the "inner world." Rational deliberation and forceful effort ordinarily prove ineffective in doing biofeedback. The more one *tries* to relax, the more, of course, he becomes tense. The outward-oriented, driving, Western tendencies are thwarted by the complacent little machine which stubbornly persists in beeping more loudly when the trainee becomes tense, regardless of his good intentions. It is not swayed by the most determined efforts and only becomes quiet when the subject finally discovers a way of letting go his muscular tension and easing into a new and deeper level of relaxation. This is seldom successful through calculated efforts since one's usual way of doing things and his usual behavior only result in maintaining his usual level of tension. A successful session with the little machine indicates that one has indeed done something "new" inside; has definitely found a way of shifting things around inside his head, permitting a new psychological organization and consequently a new degree of relaxation and freedom from tension.

Biofeedback had been given an important place in the early programs of the Himalayan Institute because the biofeedback machine served to reinforce the patient when he finally succeeded in turning his awareness inside and exploring a bit beyond the confines of his customary consciousness. It was a signpost pointing persistently to the inner world. It was a validation that one had succeeded in working in that "inner workshop" and it was a stubborn and persistent reminder when one failed to do so. The classic situation, as described in an early publication by Dr. Green of the Menninger Foundation, is that of the trainee who, after repeated attempts to quiet the biofeedback signal, became exasperated. She felt like "throwing the machine out of the window," but instead, sank back with resignation. "I can't do it," she thought, at which point the machine fell silent. She had at last "quit trying," and genuinely relaxed!

Meanwhile the Himalayan Institute had moved to a larger campus and one of its teachers who had recently completed a Ph.D. in psychology was looking for a place to do intensive meditation. It was suggested that he come to the Institute. He was provided with a private room and brought only simple, wholesome food and fresh fruit and vegetable juices. Meanwhile his work was to remain alone in quiet introspection, meditation and the practice of hatha yoga. Everyone was a bit curious about this island of solitude and silence in the midst of the busy headquarters of the Institute. After his nine day stint, however, he emerged radiant—an aura of peace and calm surrounding him. Immediately there was a list of people who wanted to come "for the nine day program." For those who came, especially those who were relatively new to yoga, biofeedback was a good introduction to the process of inner work and lectures were added to give a foundation in breathing, relaxation, meditation and the principles of nutrition. Steambaths, walks and, in some cases, work in the organic garden seemed appropriate and were soon incorporated into the program. Those who had medical problems were seen by the physicians on the staff and special methods of working with these (such as Ayurveda and homeopathy, which proved naturally compatible with meditation and yoga) were begun.

Suddenly we realized that we had already in full operation the sort of program that we had dreamed of. Here was an approach to health that was not really "medical treatment" in the usual sense. Those involved were learning to be sensitive to their bodies, to their minds, to their emotions and they were learning tools with which to regulate these. The experience was one of self-exploration, a re-assuming of responsibility for one's own well-being. Disorders of body, emotions and mind were being worked with intensively, yet the atmosphere was one of an ashram more than one of the hospital.

The whole process was more one of training rather than treatment, yet the results were gratifying. In most cases disease processes were halted and a definite restoration of health and vitality and of joy could be observed. Something happened, we were delighted to observe, when people were left on their own without anything being "done to them," but provided with the opportunity for self-examination and the techniques for regulating the breath, mental processes, and body. Physical habits were revised. Their mental components and correlates were brought into view, examined, reworked and a new psychological stance assumed. In many of the participants there was a sense of freshness, of unburdening, of being renewed.

A good example is Dr. H., a professional

therapist who came in with a complaint that he had trouble with his meditation and needed help. He also had high blood pressure, for which he had been receiving conventional medication. In the course of the physical examination some subtle indications of adrenal dysfunctioning were observed. A urine test was done and it was discovered that the adrenal hormones were below normal levels. His own statement of his problem was that he had trouble with a lack of vitality, or lack of "vital force." Somewhere in his consciousness there was a drive to make progress in meditation, yet he lacked the fire that he felt was necessary. He had spent time in an ashram in his youth and was a very sincere and dedicated person, yet it was as though he were weighted down and impeded in his progress. In the terms of Ayurveda, the traditional system of medicine in India, this seemed to make sense. *Pita*, the source of vital force which is centered at the solar plexus in the healthy, active, vibrant person was instead scattered and located near the surface where it manifested itself in terms of tension in the peripheral vessels so that high blood pressure resulted. His vitality was not at the solar plexus where it should be, rather it was in his periphery so that vascular tension was present there while inside he was weak and lax. Much of his treatment consisted in getting his energy centered again and letting the periphery relax, at which point the blood pressure began to go down and he stopped all his blood pressure medication. Finally the blood pressure was lower off the medicine than it had been on it.

To accomplish this result a variety of therapeutic techniques were used: biofeedback, using the temperature trainer, helped him learn to "warm his hands" which means relaxing and dilating the blood vessels in the extremities. Meanwhile, concentration and meditation techniques helped him learn to focus his energy at the solar plexus. Diet and exercise also contributed to an increase in his vitality. Too much food, or food that is not easily digested, overwhelms the capacity of the digestive juices, and heaviness results. In the terms of Ayurveda this would be conceptualized as a dampening or smothering of the solar plexus "fire." Similarly activity and exercise, when properly performed, activate the solar plexus and stimulate digestion promoting a sense of "energy."

But it was breathing exercises which were probably the key to coordinating his efforts and a great deal of time was spent in reeducating him in breathing patterns. In both the Ayurvedic and yogic systems of thought it is clearly understood that the mind and body are related primarily through an intermediate level of functioning, one which is little known or discussed in the West. This intermediate level of functioning is called in Sanskrit *prana*. The closest equivalent we have in English is the word "energy." This level of "energy" phenomena is very closely related to the breath.

The key to a successful Combined Therapy Program is the ability to integrate various therapeutic tools. This only becomes possible when we have a conceptual framework which is broad enough and deep enough to accommodate work on many levels: with the body, with the emotions, with the mind and even with the higher states of consciousness. Lacking such a framework, our work could easily degenerate into an uncoordinated hodge-podge of misdirected therapeutic efforts. Without the proper integration and the proper timing one therapeutic modality can actually oppose another. Lacking a comprehensive conceptual framework that would allow for a truly holistic view of the patient, most therapists realistically limit themselves to the use of one well-circumscribed and rather restricted therapeutic approach. Realistic though this may be, such a limited approach forgoes the use of other very practical therapeutic tools which could be of great benefit. Moreover, it often overlooks other very important developments going on physiologically, or mentally, or emotionally—outside the arena of "therapy." Only when one can integrate an understanding of the various levels of a person's functioning can that person be helped to reorganize, reharmonize and re-establish balance between them. The conceptual framework provided by yoga gives us a way of understanding the relationship between body, emotions and breath, mind and higher consciousness. For most persons the reworking of the relationship between the mind and the body will involve some coming to terms with this little known level of functioning called, in the East, *prana*. Those working in the Combined Therapy Program invariably begin talking in such terms. They struggle to find words but eventually they come up with some expression like "a feeling of something moving through me," or "a feeling of energy," or "a feeling of concentration or intensity," or a feeling of weakness or tiredness, or more liveliness, and so forth. In whatever terms, this business of energy becomes a concept that is real and practical and an important part of the work that they are doing. As a result of focusing on this, they discover very soon that their most powerful tool for altering it is the breath.

According to the teachings of yoga, breathing is directly related to the influx of energy into the psychophysiological system. Of course this is also recognized in Western science where we have detailed the intake of oxygen and how it brings to the cells the ability to burn fuel and produce energy. Unfortunately in Western science this has not been tied so directly to experiential events and our understanding of respiration has remained rather sterile, in the sense that it is divorced from practical, personal application. Once one becomes aware, however, of the crucial relationship between the way he breathes

and the experience of energy-like phenomena in the body
he rapidly begins to make inroads into learning to regulate
his body and emotions more effectively.

Closely related to the yogic and Ayurvedic concepts
of *prana*, or energy, is the concept of "vital force" as it
is used in the therapeutic system of homeopathy, another
medical tradition whose center is India. The homeopathic
remedy, which does not consist of pharmacologic agents
acting on biochemical processes, serves rather to alter and
reorganize the *pranic* or energy level of functioning. It
can even have repercussions on the mental level, helping
to bring unconscious material into awareness. The homeopathic remedy is the only analogue in our medical arma-
mentarium to the psychoanalytic interpretation.

Once the *pranic* level of functioning is recognized
as the crucial and strategic interface between the mind
and the body new possibilities for therapy are opened.
Tools such as breathing techniques and Ayurvedic and
homeopathic remedies become important. Moreover when
the use of the various therapeutic modalities are organized
around an awareness of this *pranic* level of functioning
they can be used synergistically rather than conflictually.
Not only are we enabled to coordinate the various aspects
of the Combined Therapy Program but this matter of
energy is a focal point for the patient/trainee's awareness.
It is, therefore, a point of intersection for therapeutic
techniques, the patient's mental and physical processes
and, always and most strategically, the use of breathing
techniques.

When therapeutic input and efforts both from the staff and the trainee are coordinated in this way it is often surprising how much reorganization and change can occur in a brief ten-day period. It is common for those who finish the program to remark on leaving, "I'm not the same person who came here." Something is learned, something is seen differently. The stance one takes in relationship to the world shifts. His inner awareness is expanded and there is no longer the same basis for the self destructive habits of physiology, of breathing, of emotions, or of mind that he persisted in before. He will never be quite the same person again, even if he tries.

Illness, whatever it is, whether it's mental, physical or emotional, is simply an opportunity for reorganization. Its appearance is an indication that the time has arrived for learning something. Now is an opportunity to make a discovery. In fact, one's whole system says rather insistently: "The opportunity is so ripe that you must stop to pay attention to this." The signal is pain.

An extraordinary thing that many find difficult to believe has occasionally occurred during the course of the Combined Therapy Program: a number of patients have come to think of pain in a positive way, as something valuable. The pain comes to be seen as a useful signal so that the patient can think "Aha! Now is the time. I've been trying to get a hold of this thing and at last the time has come." The pain means "Now I can look. Now is the time that I might catch sight of what this is all about." So that some patients come to welcome pain, not masochistically, but with curiosity and a sense of adventure, regarding it as the announcement of a long-awaited opportunity to learn something very important. Once this shift is made in one's attitude towards pain and discomfort a whole new orientation to health and illness occurs. As one's awareness of the internal world grows and one is more easily alerted to the signs of disharmony he can pick them up sooner. The job of self-examination acquires an aura of discovery and exploration. It is pursued with a sense of curiosity and adventure. One then begins to make a practice, a habit, of observing himself and learning—picking up indications that he is misusing his body in some subtle way and reading the implications of what this means in terms of his mind, his emotions, and the whole interrelated complex. The deeper he goes with this study the more he learns of himself and the better able he is to avoid difficulties and to use his energy and talents creatively. On the surface his life becomes more productive, while the adjustments and corrections in faulty habit patterns take place on subtler and deeper levels and are less obvious to those around him. Watching him from the outside one would simply say, "He's very healthy."

Such a shift in perspective on oneself is a major transition. Everything about the Combined Therapy Program is organized to encourage this. One's natural and culturally acceptable tendency to assume the passive role of "patient" is persistently ignored and all of the activities of the day, from dawn until late at night, are organized around gently promoting an increased awareness of one's inner world. Meanwhile the tools and techniques for self-discovery and self-regulation are continually offered.

Even though many participants may intellectually understand what's trying to be accomplished, they repeatedly attempt to maneuver themselves into the traditional role of passive patient. Usually several days go by, occupied with this jockeying for the patient role. This may be a time of tension, nervousness or even tears, but most often, after the third of fourth day, the participant will become quite angry. He demands: "Why didn't you tell me what this was all about? I've been wasting my time. I should have been looking at myself and learning the breathing and the meditation and the relaxation and how to manage my diet, and my exercise, etc., and already four days have gone by and I've missed so much of what I could have gotten and you should have told me what this was all about!" They're furious because they realize the enormity of the task that confronts them and the tremendous need they have for information, for skills, and for developing inner awareness. They suddenly realize the unique opportunity which they have been offered and the value of the time they have here, away from the demands of the world, with the freedom to work intensively.

When this fit of anger occurred, it was welcomed, for then we knew the major battle was won. The rest of the work the person would do for himself. The crucial shift had been made. A new stance in relation to one's health and well-being had been assumed. There was a new driver at the wheel. One more person had assumed responsibility for his health and his well-being, and had undertaken the long and arduous but fascinating task of learning how to read, interpret and regulate the inner world of body, emotions, energy and mind.

# About the Authors

## Jonathan C. Smith, Ph.D.

was born in 1946. He received his B.A. (cum laude) in psychology from Oberlin College (1968) his M.A. and Ph.D. (1973 and 1975 respectively) from Michigan State University. He was appointed Assistant Professor of Psychology at Roosevelt University Chicago (1973). He has conducted extensive studies on the psychotherapeutic potential of meditation and his research work includes eye directionality and creativity; meditation as psychotherapy; hypnosis and behavior modification techniques. He is guest reviewer for *Psychological Bulletin* and author of several papers on meditation.

## Timothy J. Thorpe, Ed.D.

is currently completing a post-doctoral internship in Counseling Psychology at Texas Tech University. His recent research work has analyzed the effects of hatha yoga and meditation on factors such as physical dysfunction, body cathexis, anxiety, depression and self-concept among drug rehabilitation patients. Receiving his masters degree in clinical psychology and his doctorate in educational psychology from the University of Tennessee, he served the same institute as a clinical psychologist and was appointed instructor of psychology at Knoxville College. A student and instructor of yoga and meditation, he has acted also as a consultant on EMG biofeedback training in the Knoxville area.

### Jean Kristeller

is a graduate student in clinical psychology and human psychophysiology at the University of Wisconsin, Madison. She has completed the research for her master's thesis and will be continuing work on her Ph.D. at Yale University, combining these interests with work in Asian Studies.

### Phil Nuernberger, Ph.D.

is director of biofeedback training and counseling psychologist for the Minneapolis Clinic of Neurology and Psychiatry. He formerly served as a counselor/therapist with the Self-Awareness Training and Therapy Institute, a professional research and training center in the Twin Cities. As a psychologist and student of meditative techniques, Dr. Nuernberger has extensive experience in yoga encounter groups and yoga counseling and conducts workshops in these areas. He was born in 1942 and educated at Southern Illinois University and the University of Minnesota where he received his doctorate in psychology. Currently a director of the Himalayan Institute, Dr. Nuernberger also serves as consultant for the Meditation Center in Minneapolis. He has co-authored *Theory and Practice of Meditation* and *Psychology East and West* and published several articles on therapeutic aspects of yoga.

### Rudolph M. Ballentine, Jr., M.D.

was born in 1941 in Columbia, South Carolina. A physician and psychiatrist, he studied psychology in the United States and France before receiving his M.D. degree from Duke University. He then travelled widely in India learning the deeper aspects of yoga and studying Ayurvedic medicine and homeopathy. He knows several languages including Hindi. A private practitioner of General and Psychosomatic Medicine, he is director of the Biofeedback-Meditation and Combined Therapy Programs of the Himalayan Institute. Dr. Ballentine lectures extensively around the country and is co-author of *Yoga and Psychotherapy* and *Science of Breath.*

### Swami Ajaya

formerly Allan Weinstock, Ph.D. is a practicing clinical psychologist and consultant to several mental health centers. He is the director of the Yoga Society of Madison, Wisconsin. Swami Ajaya is author of *Yoga Psychology* and co-author of *Yoga and Psychotherapy, Emotion to Enlightenment, Science of Breath, Theory and Practice of Meditation* and *Foundations of Eastern and Western Psychology.*

# BOOKS PUBLISHED BY THE HIMALAYAN INSTITUTE

| | |
|---|---|
| Yoga and Psychotherapy | Swami Rama, Swami Ajaya, R. Ballentine, M.D. |
| Emotion to Enlightenment | Swami Rama, Swami Ajaya |
| Freedom from the Bondage of Karma | Swami Rama |
| Book of Wisdom—Ishopanishad | Swami Rama |
| Lectures on Yoga | Swami Rama |
| Life Here and Hereafter | Swami Rama |
| Marriage, Parenthood & Enlightenment | Swami Rama |
| Meditation in Christianity | Swami Rama, et al. |
| Superconscious Meditation | Usharbudh Arya, Ph.D. |
| Philosophy of Hatha Yoga | Usharbudh Arya, Ph.D. |
| Yoga Psychology | Swami Ajaya |
| Meditational Therapy | Swami Ajaya (ed) |
| Psychology East and West | Swami Ajaya (ed) |
| Foundations of Eastern & Western Psychology | Swami Ajaya (ed) |
| Art and Science of Meditation | L. K. Misra, Ph.D. (ed) |
| Swami Rama of the Himalayas | L. K. Misra, Ph.D. (ed) |
| Theory and Practice of Meditation | R. M. Ballentine, M.D. (ed) |
| Science of Breath | R. M. Ballentine, M.D. (ed) |
| Joints & Glands Exercises | R. M. Ballentine, M.D. (ed) |
| Science Studies Yoga | James Funderburk, Ph.D. |
| Hatha Yoga Manual I | Samskrti and Veda |
| The Swami and Sam (for children) | Brandt Dayton |
| Himalayan Mountain Cookery | Mrs. R. Ballentine, Sr. (ed) |
| The Yoga Way Cookbook | Friends of the Institute |